THE SEVEN-DAY WEEKEND

THE SEVEN-DAY WEEKEND

Changing the Way Work Works

Ricardo Semler

PORTFOLIO

For Rogério Ottolia,

who left much too early

but will stay in Semco's heart forever

PORTFOLIO
Published by the Penguin Group
Penguin Group (USA) Inc., 375 Hudson Street, New York, New York 10014, U.S.A.
Penguin Books Ltd, 80 Strand, London WC2R ORL, England
Penguin Books Australia Ltd, 250 Camberwell Road, Camberwell,
Victoria 3124, Australia
Penguin Books Canada Ltd, 10 Alcorn Avenue, Toronto, Ontario, Canada M4V 3B2
Penguin Books India (P) Ltd, 11 Community Centre, Panchsheel Park,
New Delhi – 110 017, India
Penguin Books (N.Z.) Ltd, Cnr Rosedale and Airborne Roads, Albany, Auckland,
New Zealand
Penguin Books (South Africa) (Pty) Ltd, 24 Sturdee Avenue, Rosebank,
Johannesburg 2196, South Africa

Penguin Books Ltd, Registered Offices: 80 Strand, London WC2R ORL, England

First American edition
Published in 2004 by Portfolio,
a member of Penguin Group (USA) Inc.

10   9   8   7   6   5   4   3   2   1

CIP data available

ISBN 1-59184-026-0

This book is printed on acid-free paper. ∞

Printed in the United States of America
Set in Dante
Designed by Richard Oriolo

ACKNOWLEDGMENTS

TO THOSE FEISTY PROS without whom this book would never have seen the light of day: foremost Roger Gittines, with his dry humor, his laser sharp eye, and his cryptic comments; my editors Adrian Zackheim and Stephanie Land—where all fights were good fights and enthusiasm never slackened; and lastly but never leastly, Heather Schroder, my agent at ICM and a friend for all seasons of publishing.

At home, Fernanda, with the warmest factory-built heart I've seen, who cheerled when the team was losing and who is in the process of redesigning my own heart. She's the only e-mail that comes with Un-attachments.

To my four-year-old Felipe, an angel of inspiration, who picks up his toy computer and says he has to work now. The thought of him makes me break into a wide smile every time.

To Curt, a firm handshake (and a peck on the cheek) across space and time for the fifty-year anniversary of Semco— shaped (so far) half and half by two Semlers.

To my kin at Semco, a big Brazilian *abraço*.

CONTENTS

FOREWARNING

"Sometimes I sits and thinks, sometimes I just sits."
—SATCHEL PAIGE

NEVER MIND THE CHEESE—who moved my weekend?

I'm serious. Where did it go? One minute Saturday and Sunday formed an oasis for rest, relaxation, and rejuvenation. The next thing we know the cell phone is ringing, e-mail is piling up, and the fax machine is vomiting paper onto the floor. Paradise lost. Welcome to the seven-day workweek.

I've got a much better idea, though, one that I've been road testing now for many years: the seven-day weekend. If the workweek is going to slop over into the weekend—and there's no hope of stopping that from happening—why can't the weekend, with its precious restorative moments of playtime, my time, and our time, spill over into the workweek?

It can and, I believe, must happen. In fact, the seven-day weekend is already happening at Semco, an unusual company that I'll introduce you to in the pages ahead. What you are about to read is a combination of a political manifesto, a business case history, and an anthropological study. Before you shudder, groan, and heave the book across the room, I'll hasten to add that it's also a road map to personal and business success. We have to find a better way for work to work. The seven-day workweek is shaping up as a personal, societal, and business disaster. It robs people of passion and pleasure, destroys family and community stability, and sets up business organizations to ultimately fail once they've burned out their employees and burned through ever more manipulative and oppressive strategies.

The seven-day weekend approach is an alternative that bridges the gap between the airy theories of workplace democracy and the nitty-gritty practice of running a profitable business. I warn you, it's messy, inefficient, and hugely rewarding. I've chosen the metaphor of the seven-day weekend as an anchor. You're welcome to take the turn of phrase literally or figuratively. But don't kid yourself: I'm not talking about abolishing work. A seven-day weekend, however pleasant a fantasy of endless strolls on the beach, will mix work time with personal time in new and possibly disconcerting ways. Don't worry, though—it also doesn't imply that you'll be forever tethered to your laptop. Your first reaction may be dismay at the loss of your conventional weekend; after all, we naïvely define weekends as free time, personal days, idleness. But that definition is outdated. The traditional weekend and workweeks ended long ago. This book faces that fact and explores ways of making work more fun, and of finding a balance between work and private passions, so both can be significantly gratifying.

To do that, we must reorganize the workplace, both physically and culturally. At Semco, we've spent twenty-five years doing just that, primarily by constantly questioning the way we do things. When we started, everyone said we wouldn't last. Now Semco employs three thousand people working in three countries in manufacturing, professional services, and high-tech software. But even now, I continue to hear that our experiments could never work anywhere else. Yet we go on proving that in redistributing the weekend across the workweek, our employees find balance and Semco makes money. In that regard alone, we are an excellent business case study. We fit neatly into any MBA examination of success.

It's very simple—the repetition, boredom, and aggravation that too many people accept as an inherent part of working can be replaced with joy, inspiration, and freedom.

That's what I wish for everyone who reads this book.

RICARDO SEMLER
(Lying in a hammock with a laptop and my little boy,
having fed the ducks at a nearby pond)
On a Monday in May

ANY DAY

- Ask why?
- Give up control.
- Change the way work works.

I'M A CATALYST, AND that's why I was on a ten-hour Varig flight from Sao Paulo to New York, fastening my seat belt and making sure the tray table was in an upright and locked position for landing.

You read that correctly the first time—catalyst. By definition a catalyst, usually an enzyme, initiates a reaction. The way I handle the role is by broaching weird ideas and asking dumb questions. Strictly speaking, I'm a highly evolved CEO, as in "Chief Enzyme Officer."

As such, I was fated to make the trip the moment I casually said to my Semco colleagues, "I bet we can get the phone number of the Rockefeller Group by calling information. It must be listed, don't you think?" It was. Like a good enzyme, I even offered to dial the number, too, since I was perched on the front edge of my desk, a favorite spot that allows me to get to my feet quickly to end meetings that start to drag.

"Oh, Mr. Mirante, you mean," the company operator said when I blandly asked the name of Cushman & Wakefield's president, pretending that I had just suffered a slight memory lapse.

"Yes, Mr. Mirante. Would you ring his office please?" Cushman & Wakefield is the commercial real estate arm of the Rockefeller Group. When Arthur Mirante's secretary picked up the phone, I told her that I was calling from Brazil. For some reason that worked magic—maybe she had a secret fantasy about attending Carnival in Rio—the next thing I knew President Mirante himself was on the line.

It took about three minutes; record time, considering he didn't have a clue about me or my agenda. I explained who I was—leaving out the bit about being a catalyst—and suggested that we get together face-to-face to discuss a business proposition. My new friend, Arthur, agreed without pressing for details.

Now, standing in the cab rank at JFK Airport, having been stranded by a no-show limo driver, I experienced my latest pang of misgivings: "Cushman & Wakefield is going to agree to partner with an obscure Brazilian company? Get serious, Ricardo. This is one weird idea that's about to fizzle."

A cacophony of Indian sitar music provided the sound

track for my trip through Queens to midtown Manhattan. I asked the cabbie to turn it down, but he couldn't hear me over the noise. Ears ringing, I got out on Fifth Avenue, wended my way past the famous ice-skating rink (in springtime hibernation), noted the façade of Radio City Music Hall with its flashy neon marquee, and entered the high-rise domain of one of the world's largest real estate management firms.

I whisked through the revolving door and sailed straight past the security desk without stopping, affecting the bearing of a Rockefeller scion (Rocky Ricardo?), a little game I used to play prior to 9/11. I was pretty good at looking like I knew where I was going; guards rarely stopped me for ID or destination checks. (Alas, those days are over in the United States.) The elevator ride to the thirty-sixth floor gave me just enough time to review my predicament without triggering full-fledged qualms. Surrounded by hundreds of engineers, brokers, and high-end property managers, I was about to propose that Semco, a company with zero experience in real estate, join forces with the Rockefeller family to handle the nitty-gritty business of facility management in Brazil and the rest of Latin America.

I introduced myself to the receptionist and moments later was sitting on an opulent silk-covered sofa wondering if I had been wise to wear jeans and a blazer. The doubts about my attire were almost instantly reinforced when into the office suite strode Arthur Mirante II, tall and stylishly draped in an elegant, Italian-designer suit that reeked of many fittings by cadres of attentive artisans.

His firm handshake and warm, open smile put me at ease.

I reminded myself that I was supposed to be having fun and so, presumably, was he. I noticed that he gave my jeans a quick sideways glance of appraisal. We bantered a few moments about not usually setting up meetings based on a three-minute phone call, or flying ten hours on the same flimsy pretext, and then quickly got down to business. I summarized my proposal, emphasizing Semco's background in manufacturing and maintenance, but Mirante looked disappointed.

"I'm sorry you came all the way for this, then," he said. "The problem is we don't make much money in that business. It mainly supports our other real estate interests."

I countered that I was confident we could make a business out of it in Brazil. Mirante asked if I really wouldn't be more interested in the brokerage business. I confessed that my knowledge of real estate started and ended with buying my home.

With that the executive shrugged and took me to see his facility management people. Afterward, I suggested that each of us put up $2,000 to cover the legal expenses of establishing the venture. We'd be fifty-fifty partners. Arthur agreed, we shook hands, and off I went in a hurry to pick up tickets to the New York Philharmonic, have lunch with the writer Peter Carey, and hit the legendary Strand bookstore for three hours of browsing their stock of used and remaindered books.

That was April of 1993. A year later, the Semco Cushman & Wakefield joint venture employed 150 people and did $4 million in business. Today, it employs 1,300 people and has gross revenues of more than $65 million.

Why am I telling you this story, much less starting a book with it? For one thing, you couldn't concoct a more outrageous and unlikely combination. Staid, proper, blue-blooded Cushman & Wakefield united with casual, off-the-wall, planning averse, nearly anything goes Semco. Talk about an odd couple! But I contend the strangeness is its strength. There's resiliency, flexibility, and sustainability to the venture that would be lacking in a more conventional pairing.

Even so, my purpose is much more subversive than merely recounting an unlikely success story. I believe the old way of doing business is dying, and the sooner it's dead and buried the better off we all will be. Incendiary words, yet Semco's alliance with Cushman & Wakefield, as well as other joint ventures that I will describe shortly, suggests that the transition from the old to the new can be hugely profitable and not nearly as socially disruptive as might be feared at first. On the contrary, the path Semco has been blazing for more than twenty years has led to an unprecedented record of innovation, customer satisfaction, growth, and an end to repressive command-and-control management practices that cause much labor unrest and personal misery, from the top to the bottom of many organizations.

One of the recurring themes of this book is the need—the absolute necessity—to give up control in order to cope with changes that are transforming the way we live and work. As counterintuitive as that sounds, it does not contradict the experience and values at the core of free market, democratic capitalism. I don't want to speak for Arthur Mirante, who is indeed an excellent friend and wonderful partner, but it seems to me that something in my casual, drive-by approach appealed to his entrepreneurial instincts. He was willing to take a chance—to give up control. Isn't that what entrepreneurs do? They're flexible, intuitive, nondogmatic; they take risks, make money, and have fun.

But many entrepreneurs—be they leaders of great or small enterprises—can't bring themselves to let go. They probably would have shown me the door, and turned away from a $65 million venture. I believe the obsession with control is a delusion and, increasingly, a fatal business error. The more we grab for it, the more it slips away, and ever more desperate measures are applied, spawning Enrons, WorldComs, and hosts of lower profile disasters. As the control mechanism grows harsher and harsher, what's lost is the central purpose of the business, any business—a satisfying, worthwhile life for those involved and a reasonable reward for their investment and hard work.

The seven-day weekend is Semco's way of getting out of the control business and back to our central purpose.

SHAPING SEMCO

Nearly twenty years ago a prominent Brazilian politician invited me to the far north of Brazil for a conference. Senator Jose Macedo, a wonderful self-made man, had begun his working life as a soap salesman. By the time I met him, he was a billionaire in the flour, biscuit, beer, and car dealership businesses.

I spoke at the conference for an hour about Semco and its unusual practices, and then Senator Macedo opened the question-and-answer session. Sitting in the first row, he looked back over his shoulder at the hundreds of people who filled the hot, humid auditorium and asked, "Mr. Semler, before answering other questions, can you please tell us what planet you're from?" It took several minutes for the room to quiet down, and I can still hear the good-natured laughter.

In case you're tempted to ask the same question after reading a few more pages of this book, I suggest that we first pursue another line of inquiry that might prove more helpful and less inflammatory. The question that I have in mind is, what is Semco?

The only problem is that now I have to come up with an answer. If you ask me to describe it in conventional business terms, I'd have to admit I have no idea what business Semco is in. For years, I have resisted defining Semco for a simple reason: Once you say what business you're in, you create boundaries for your employees, you restrict their thinking and give them a reason to ignore new opportunities. "We're not in that business," they'll say.

Instead of dictating Semco's identity, I let our employees shape it with their individual efforts, interests, and initiatives.

You probably don't like my answer, and I don't blame you. I'll try again from another angle. Instead of explaining what Semco does, I'll take a run at what it doesn't do.

Semco has no official structure. It has no organizational chart. There's no business plan or company strategy, no two-year or five-year plan, no goal or mission statement, no long-term budget. The company often does not have a fixed CEO. There are no vice presidents or chief officers for information technology or operations. There are no standards or practices. There's no human resources department. There are no career plans, no job descriptions or employee contracts. No one approves reports or expense accounts. Supervision or monitoring of workers is rare indeed.

Most important, success is not measured only in profit and growth.

Strange, eh? My summary may make Semco sound like a company with an offbeat management style that wouldn't succeed anywhere else. Nevertheless, hundreds of corporate leaders from around the world have visited Sao Paulo to find out what makes us tick. The visitors are curious about Semco because they want what we have—huge growth in spite of a fluctuating economy, unique market niches, rising profits, highly motivated employees, low turnover, diverse products, and service areas.

Our visitors want to understand how Semco has increased its annual revenue between 1994 and 2003 from $35 million a year to $212 million when I—the company's largest shareholder—rarely attend meetings and almost never make decisions. They want to know how my employees, with a show of hands, can veto new product ideas or scrap whole business ventures.

This book will explain the straightforward philosophies and practices that make Semco one of the world's most unusual workplaces. Be warned—many of our basic tenets fly in the face of even the most progressive business owners or managers. Our "architecture" is really the sum of all the conventional business practices we avoid.

It's our lack of formal structure, our willingness to let workers follow their interests and their instincts when choosing jobs or projects.

It's our insistence that workers seek personal challenges and satisfaction before trying to meet the company's goals.

It's our commitment to encouraging employees to ramble through their day or week so that they will meander into new ideas and new business opportunities.

It's our philosophy of embracing democracy and open communication, and inciting questions and dissent in the workplace.

On-the-job democracy isn't just a lofty concept but a better, more profitable way to do things. We all demand democracy in every other aspect of our lives and culture. People are considered adults in their private lives, at the bank, at their children's schools, with family and among friends—so why are they suddenly treated like adolescents at work? Why can't workers be involved in choosing their own leaders? Why shouldn't they manage themselves? Why can't they speak up—challenge, question, share information openly?

Semco's glass and steel high-rise headquarters is a far cry from the gritty industrial shop floor that my father, Antonio Curt Semler, founded in 1954. It started not long after he moved to Brazil from Argentina, having emigrated before that from his native Vienna. He patented a centrifuge for separating oils, and with that started his own small machine shop, choosing its name from a contraction of Semler & Company. Soon Semco was a $2 million a year business. Then, in the late 1960s, my father formed a partnership with two British marine pump manufacturers, and Semco quickly became a major supplier to the Brazilian shipbuilding industry.

For the next twenty-five years, Semco built marine pumps, and its name became synonymous with the shipping industry. It could also have been synonymous with rigidity and tradition. When I was still quite young, my father assumed that I would take over Semco. I wasn't anywhere near as certain as he was. I spent many youthful years in a rock band and one miserable summer as an intern in Semco's purchasing department. After that, I wondered, "How can I spend the rest of my life doing this? How can I stomach years of babysitting people to make sure they clock in on time? Why is this worth doing?"

When I told my father about my qualms, he reassured me with "that'll pass, young man," or "I, too, was once like you." Of course that only made matters worse. Instead, I began to wonder if it was possible to foster change by creating an entirely new kind of organization.

The answer was yes, but it involved a deceptively simple principle—relinquishing control in order to institute true democracy at Semco. And that is very complicated indeed. Convinced that my family wouldn't let me have free rein at Semco, I spent a year investigating a faltering ladder manufacturer. I was then twenty-one and preferred the prospect of a small, dangerous venture before I made a commitment to family interests. On the day I was to sign the final papers to acquire the ladder company, my father called me and proposed a deal.

After much debate and negotiation, we agreed that I'd take over Semco, and he would step back and allow me to remake the company as I saw fit. I was so young that no one at Semco took the news seriously. Clovis Bojikian, today one of five senior Semco managers and our venerable human resources guru, remembers coming to Semco for an interview shortly after I took over.

"They put me in a room, and a boy arrived," Clovis says now. "I thought he was a messenger. He was about my son's age. He sat down and started to ask me questions, and it was Ricardo Semler."

Within days of taking over, I fired two-thirds of my father's most senior managers outright. A risky move that I felt was necessary to quickly implement reforms without foot dragging from the entrenched executives. I then spent the next two decades questioning,

> EVEN THOUGH OUR WORKERS CAN VETO A DEAL OR CLOSE A FACTORY WITH A SHOW OF HANDS, SEMCO GROWS AN AVERAGE OF 40 PERCENT A YEAR AND HAS ANNUAL REVENUE OF MORE THAN $212 MILLION.

challenging, and dismantling the traditional business practices at Semco.

TODAY, I CAN HONESTLY say that our growth, profit, and the number of people we employ are secondary concerns. Outsiders clamor to know these things because they want to quantify our business. These are the yardsticks they turn to first. That's one reason we're still privately held. I don't want Semco to be burdened with the ninety-day mind-set of most stock market analysts. It would undermine our solidity and force us to dance to a tune we don't really want to hear—a Wall Street waltz that starts each day with an opening bell and ends with the thump of the closing gavel.

Thanks, but no thanks. We generate enough of our own cash, and we're growing nearly 40 percent a year without public investment. Yes, we're successful by market standards—we've grown, we've made more money, and we've added employees. But that success means little to me if it's measured only in those terms. Sure, it's wonderful to have money. Yet it doesn't change how we feel about getting out of bed in the morning, going to work, and performing a job day after day.

The principles we now practice have resulted in tremendous growth: Semco has gone from my father's peak of $4 million a year to $212 million in annual revenue in 2003. My father's ninety employees have increased to nearly three thousand. We've moved from industrial manufacturing to services to high technology without giving up any earlier businesses.

Semco workers make money for the company and take a good chunk of it for themselves in a profit-sharing plan. Most important, they make it the kind of organization that people clamor to work for, a place where turnover is negligible.

Semco's experience befits more than just business. It's germane to any organization where flesh-and-blood realities of the workplace guide how people interact. The type and size of the organization is irrelevant—that's why Semco practices have been adopted at schools, hospitals, police departments, and large and small companies around the world.

Along the way, I've lost sight of what defines Semco. That's not because it's too big to manage or because I've stepped back too far from day-to-day operations. I don't want to know where Semco is headed. It doesn't unnerve me to see nothing on the company's horizon. I want Semco and its employees to ramble through their days, to use instinct, opportunity, and ingenuity to choose projects and ventures.

Fortunately, my convictions have borne results that business people value, and more important, can understand: sustainability, productivity, profit, growth, and new ventures. These are all by-products of running a company where employees are encouraged to establish their own sense of balance.

And the increasingly popular concept of work/life balance is not all that we seek. Balance also ensues when people are given room to explore so they can find out where their talents and interests lie and merge their personal aspirations with the goals of the company. Once employees feel challenged, invigorated, and productive, their efforts will naturally translate into profit and growth for the organization. That's what the Semco way is all about.

A FEDERATION

I'll bet you still want to know what Semco does. Okay, we have ten companies, give or take. I'm not sure, because they come and go; we've had a minimum of five for twenty years. We also have six Internet companies, so we could claim sixteen units, but we don't know how many of those will survive, or in what form.

At the risk of offering a description, Semco is a federation of businesses with a minimum common denominator. What I mean is we are not monolithic, yet there are common themes and threads uniting us. All our business units are highly engineered, premium providers and market leaders in their niches. We haven't ventured into any of them by chance.

The first, the industrial machinery unit, is what's left of my father's original business. It began with marine pumps and moved into industrial mixers, and now produces only high-tech mixing equipment—the kind of complex, engineered industrial mixers used for pharmaceuticals and at candy factories.

The second unit is SemcoBAC; a partnership with Baltimore Air Coil in the United States. Essentially, we make cooling towers for commercial properties. The third company is Cushman & Wakefield Semco. The fourth business unit is Semco Johnson Controls—a partnership with Johnson Controls, a $16 billion world leader in facility management to handle large properties like hospitals, airports, hotels, and huge factories. Then there's ERM. We added this unit in 1996 in partnership with Environmental Resources Management, one of the world's premier environmental consulting companies.

Finally, we have Semco Ventures, our nod to the Internet and our high-tech ventures unit; SemcoHR, which manages the outsourcing of HR activities for large companies; and Semco-RGIS, our inventory control firm.

Semco's ten (eleven, twelve . . . who's counting?) units are very diverse; in fact, you might wonder how such industries came to be part of the same business. But a closer look will reveal a hidden synergy that satisfies three basic criteria when we consider a new venture. First, we look for complexity, which usually means "highly engineered." Everything has a high entry barrier of complexity. If a new business isn't difficult for us and for others to break into, then we're not interested.

Second, we demand that in each of our markets, we be the premium player. We want to offer a high-end product or service. That means we're always more expensive because we provide the premium that stretches what the customer will pay. And third, we want a unique niche in the market, one that makes us a major player in any given industry. To us, this follows naturally from the first two requirements. We want to be only in businesses where our disappearance would cause our disheartened customers to complain loudly. They'd survive, but they'd have substantial difficulty moving on.

> EMPLOYEES MUST BE FREE
> TO QUESTION, TO ANALYZE,
> TO INVESTIGATE; AND A
> COMPANY MUST BE FLEXIBLE
> ENOUGH TO LISTEN TO THE
> ANSWERS.

All of our products and services meet these criteria, and we leverage the power of our units. For example, Wal-Mart has gradually become a customer of four of our units—we count their inventory, manage their cooling towers, administer their buildings and warehouses, and conduct environmental site investigation and remediation.

Other clients like GM, BankBoston, and Unilever have become customers of multiple Semco units. This isn't unusual for us. The point of entry may change, but our objective remains the same—synergy.

Whichever unit serves as the point of entry, it soon finds business opportunities for the others. Signing on with a client is usually our biggest hurdle, since we are more expensive than our competitors. Once a customer is on board, however, we rarely have operational problems, we rarely abandon a customer, and they rarely leave us. Repeat customers represent some 80 percent of our annual revenue. I can count on my fingers the number of clients who have dropped us in twenty years of business.

THE WHYWAY

The secret? If we have a cardinal strategy that forms the bedrock for all our practices, it may be this:

Ask why.

Ask it all the time, ask it any day, every day, and always ask it three times in a row.

This doesn't come naturally. People are conditioned to recoil from questioning too much. First, it can be perceived as rude. Second, it can be dangerous, implying that we're ignorant or uninformed. Third, it means everything we think we know may turn out to be incorrect or incomplete. Last, management is usually threatened by the prospect of employees who question continually. But mostly, it means putting aside all the rote or pat answers that have resulted from what I call "calcified" thinking, that state of mind where ideas have become so hardened that they're no longer of any use. Employees must be free to question, to analyze, to investigate; and a company must be flexible enough to listen to the answers. Those habits are the key to longevity, growth, and profit.

Asking why in this manner is also refreshingly childish, therefore of essence. When I tell my four-year-old something and he asks why, I have a good adult, pat answer. Then he asks a second why, and I'm in a bit of trouble. By the third why there is no solution but to buy him an ice cream.

Thus it is at Semco meetings. Sometimes they are like scenes from an overly artsy foreign film—we address the same subject again and again. The angles are quirky and the focus fuzzy. We ask why repeatedly. And nothing gets carved in stone. That's because as a company we hate written plans. People will follow a plan like a Pied Piper—mindlessly, with no thought as to the final destination.

At Semco, we often jot down generic ideas and broad numbers so we can visualize the dimensions of a new product or service. Then we throw those notes away. At the next meeting on the same idea, we'll start over, without the benefit of the original notes. That way we cannot fall into the trap of "fixed assumptions." It forces us to reconsider all the variables.

When an executive is new to Semco, he or she will often stammer: "But we already decided that at the last meeting," or "Why are we going over this again, instead of forging ahead?" I'm sure it's frustrating for them. But when they watch the process unfold, and if they listen to their colleagues asking why, they'll see how it allows no stone to be left unturned. Soon they're roaring down the whyway with the rest of us.

In the 1990s, our philosophies, practices, and high speed merges onto the whyway attracted attention. Six thousand people have written to us, curious about Semco, and hundreds of newspaper and magazine articles have featured our company. BBC television and dozens of other TV programs have profiled us. I've given nearly three hundred speeches to companies, conferences, charitable groups, youth groups, and universities such as Stanford, Harvard, MIT, the London School of Economics, and INSEAD. Semco is a case study at 76 universities, and texts of our organizational practices are required reading at 271 other schools. Sixteen master's and doctoral candidates have made Semco the subject of their theses.

And the first book about Semco, *Maverick,* was on bestseller lists in twelve countries and sold more than one million copies even though we had yet to really prove ourselves, let alone demonstrate staying power.

But the point I'm making is that all of this demonstrates a bona fide interest in Semco. Yet when visitors learn that our economic success requires replacing control and structure with democracy in the workplace —well, often those starry-eyed visiting executives go home with second thoughts and never get around to making it happen in their workplaces.

Why is that? Why do these visitors shy away from practices that are hugely successful both in terms of the bottom line and in the pursuit and attainment of personal happiness? And for the third consecutive why, why do organizations and their leaders cling to a rigid form of command and control that is at odds with the values of personal freedom that they cherish?

Don't tell me that the answer is profits. Semco makes plenty of money. But let the whys linger and ripen. The answers— or more whys—will come in due course. We need to first walk through the seven-day weekend that is the metaphor for the Semco way. Oh, did I forget to mention that among those things Semco doesn't do is a Monday to Friday workweek? If rock climbing is more inviting on a Wednesday morning than a budget planning meeting, then break out the rope and pitons. If lighter traffic on a Saturday afternoon makes the commute to the office bearable, go for it. Yet, the seven-day weekend is more than permission to play hooky. It's about creating an atmosphere and culture that grants permission to employees to be men and women in full for seven days a week. Why should the fun, fulfillment, and freedom stop first thing Monday morning and be on hold until Friday night? And that's one why that we will revisit as the book moves forward because I believe no one can afford, can endure, or can stomach leaving half a life in the parking lot when she or he goes to work. It's a lousy way to live and a lousy way to work.

Although I still can't definitely answer the question about what Semco does do, I can say we've changed the way work works and improved the quality of our lives—and so can you.

- **Why does a workweek have five days?**

- **Why does a weekend have two days?**

- **Why nine-to-five?**

SUNDAY

- Answer your e-mail.
- Be idle.
- Form new habits.

SOMETIMES AT BUSINESS WORKSHOPS that I conduct, I ask participants to write down what they would rather be doing at that moment. I've never had someone write: "Nothing. I signed up for this sucker, so this is exactly how I want to spend my time." They always write fishing, golfing, playing with the kids, digging in the garden, or even answering e-mail.

But shouldn't they say the workshop is the only place they want to be? Why is it a given that work is the last thing someone wants to do? Instead, we lament being robbed of freedom, and it is that lamentation that hints at an answer to these questions.

Freedom is an empty word without "free time." I don't mean chore time, errand time, homework time. Free time must be unencumbered by a to-do list. It is epitomized by idleness, otherwise time is not free if it belongs to something or someone else. Robbed of idleness, free time is stripped of its restorative powers.

Work is so intense these days, so all-consuming that it is the arch enemy of free time. It looms like a dark castle on the distant horizon, symbolizing oppression. My workshop question taps an instinctive awareness of that fact and generates an almost romantic longing for free time and a preference to be somewhere else even if it means also forfeiting idleness in the form of a weekend off that is actually a weekend on steroids.

Consequently, we no longer grasp the difference between leisure time and being idle. Western society is highly structured and action-oriented. If you go to the beach, you don't spend the day doing nothing. Within half an hour you're reading, walking, collecting seashells, swimming, fretting about your tan or your overexposure to the sun. Most of us have to keep one eye on our children while slathering on sunscreen and planning dinner. Idleness, in this case, is really just a change of scenery. There's no true opportunity to sit back, relax, and let the mind wander. That's too bad. An idle, wandering mind is not the devil's playground, as the Puritans believed, but a garden of rejuvenation, growth, and contemplation. Even when we set

> WE NO LONGER GRASP THE DIFFERENCE BETWEEN LEISURE TIME AND BEING IDLE.

weekends aside to do what we want, we often spend most of Saturday and Sunday engaged in chores, personal tasks, and other obligations. In my book, that's still work—you're just not getting paid for it, and you're certainly not relaxing.

We insist that spending quality time with our family is the number one priority. And a study done in 2001 would seem to back that up. It reported that kids between the ages of three and twelve spent thirty-one hours a week with their mothers and twenty-three hours with their fathers. They had more time with their parents than children twenty years before. But the study also found that the increase was due to the hours the kids spent sitting in traffic with Mom while she ferried them to soccer games, music lessions, and day camp, or from errand to errand. Is this the kind of quality time we had in mind? Are any of us better off for it?

And now, technology permits work to seep increasingly into the gaps between weekend activities. We can work at home, be tracked on our cell phones at the beach, read reports sent to us anywhere via e-mail. Technology has made us accessible twenty-four hours a day, seven days a week. It has no respect for the weekend or for the sanctity of a Sunday afternoon. Once, it was possible to completely avoid contact from the working world simply by refusing to give out a home phone number. Now, e-mail is coming to TV! When a football game is on and a telltale beeping announces an e-mail with an exclamation mark, will anyone be able to ignore the message and go on watching the action?

Technology has encroached so deeply into our lives that I believe we must make deliberate efforts to beat it back. Changing the way work works is the way to go. People should be encouraged to rearrange their week, drop the traditional notions of a workweek and a weekend, and divide the seven days among company time, personal time, and idleness (free time). Then they should look for more efficient ways to manage their time. Instead of wasting it in rush hour traffic, rearrange your schedule to work when most other people don't. Run errands on a quiet Monday, particularly if you've spent your Sunday answering e-mail.

It's in your best interest, and your company's best interest, to understand this. Anyone who can eliminate the stress of an overbooked schedule, arrange a workweek to sleep according to biorhythms rather than a time clock, and enjoy a sunny Monday on the beach after working through a chilly Sunday, will be a much more productive worker. It will ultimately benefit organizations because employees will find equilibrium in their professional, personal, and spiritual lives. This isn't just an avant-garde approach to running a company. It's a sound strategy for business success and gaining competitive advantage.

To put it another way, people who have learned to answer e-mails on Sunday evenings also need to learn how to go to the movies on Monday afternoons. To get to that point, they must discover that happiness, contentment, and inner peace do not come from joining the rat race in order to acquire DVD recorders, big screen TVs, cable hookups, expensive cars, and big houses, much less private helicopters and pilots. Even so, I'm not preaching antimaterialism. We do, however, desperately need a better understanding of the purpose of work, and to organize the workplace and the workweek accordingly. Without it, the purpose of work degenerates to empty materialism on one side and knee-jerk profiteering on the other.

Every time I propose reinventing the workweek to allow more freedom and flexibility, there's a skeptic in the front row rolling his eyes as if to say, "Wait a minute, if I let employees come and go as they please, half of them won't show and nothing will get done." But that's not going to happen; people want to work when work is not the enemy of personal freedom and legitimate self-interest. Let's say you declare every day a Sunday, and leave people alone with their toys and accessories. You wouldn't be granting them automatic peace and contentment. The lack of challenge, meaning, and purpose would be suffocating. Human beings thrive on being productive, on working toward goals, on providing for their families, on building a future—just don't ask them to do it all the time and without the freedom to say, "Now, I need time for me."

What's important to understand about the seven-day weekend is that by redesigning the architecture of time, we can make room for work, leisure, and idleness. All three can coexist and harmonize together to produce happiness and a sense of purpose.

Since work is so ubiquitous, we have to find ways to make it fulfilling and to curb its propensity to suck up all the available hours. Let's start by borrowing a term that's usually associated with Eastern religions—symbiosis. Roughly speaking it means "a living together," and implies that the combination is mutually beneficial, if not downright blissful. For instance, the "work" of a Tibetan monk exists symbiotically with his intimate beliefs and sense of purpose. Now there's a happy, contented man, at peace with himself and the world around him—or so it seems.

While I may not be sure about the monk's soul, I am certain that we all need that kind of symbiosis. First we have to face up to the technological changes that have occurred and reorganize daily life with them in mind. Sociologists might argue that eliminating fixed days and events and creating a world of constant and sudden change would make people insecure, perhaps unhinged. But a seven-day weekend (and implicitly a seven-day workweek) doesn't mean that the regular Sunday lunch with the parents will cease to exist or that weekly Mass will be on erratic days. People will maintain their important routines, just as they do now without feeling like the Sunday lunch is a burden they'd like to cancel. The rest of the time, they'll create other fixed events like Marcio Batoni, the CEO of Semco RGIS, who has a regular Tuesday afternoon movie date with his wife.

Semco is bucking not only the traditional business model, we're resisting a code of behavior at the very core of Western culture. No wonder our ideals are hard for outsiders and other companies to embrace.

At Semco we insist that our people form new habits. They start by adopting one abiding principle: Avoid routine and steer clear of habit. To that end, we've eliminated some of the more familiar, dependable structures of most organizations. We tossed the rigorous nine to five, Monday through Friday schedule out the window. Dumped any requirement that employees work only in a specific office, factory, or other piece of Semco real estate. And we are also dismantling our own headquarters in favor of satellite and portable offices.

When Semco first introduced flexible work schedules and impermanent offices in the mid-1980s, virtually everyone predicted we'd fail immediately. Couldn't we see, the skeptics asked, that people need regular hours and regular contact with each other, that they need to speak to each other face-to-face, and know when and where to find each other? They'd need a common meeting ground, the proverbial gathering around the water cooler or cappuccino machine. Nowhere was this more obvious and critical than on the assembly line, the naysayers said. So when we expanded flextime to include assembly-line workers, all intellectual hell broke loose. That was taking it too far, we heard—we were ignoring the basic requirements of a shop floor. Of course an assembly line cannot have flextime, people hollered. And we just asked, "Why?"

"Isn't it obvious?" they said. If workers weren't working at the same time, the assembly lines would grind to a halt. Okay, we knew that, but so did the adults who work on it. And why would they jeopardize their output, their jobs? If they didn't care if the assembly line moved or stopped, then we'd have a much graver problem, and the sooner we found out the better. I was confident that our assembly-line workers would implement the flextime schedule in a way that kept operations running smoothly.

In case I was crazy, it was agreed that a committee would meet twice a day for the first month, once a day for two months thereafter, and finally twice a week for a year, to deal with any problems, stoppages, and conflicts that the doubters were confident would inevitably occur.

That committee never met. The day before the program began, people turned to their left and their right and asked what time the others would be coming in the next morning. End of story.

TRUST IN ADULT BEHAVIOR

Now Semco employees are free to customize their workdays, to come in earlier or later than traditional schedules. The hours they work are determined by their self-interest, not by company dictates. They're the best judges of the amount of time and the proper place necessary to get their job done.

Yet people continue to assume that chaos would ensue if everyone were left to choose their own work time. Journalists tell me that newspapers wouldn't be published some days, doctors say that operations would be canceled due to an anesthetist who didn't show up, actors insist that their play's curtain wouldn't rise, and transport specialists maintain that the subway would be shut down.

Nonsense.

Do we really believe that responsible adults, whether interested or not, committed to the company or service or not, would simply fail to show up after promising to do so; that a journalist who understands the urgency of deadlines will go to the movies while the presses are standing still, waiting for his article to be submitted; that the woman who studied anesthetics for years will simply roll over in bed, thinking that the patient should have taken more care with his cholesterol? Or that actors who chose the theater will leave the public waiting in vain for the curtain to rise, and a subway car driver will shrug and take his granddaughter to school while people stand on the platform, looking into a dark tunnel for a train that never arrives? Come on. What a disheartening view of humankind.

The same prophets of doom made the same arguments when we first proposed twenty years ago that people could work away from the office. They made two false assumptions: The first is that home will replace the office as the only work location. That's just not true. Our people work in Semco's satellite offices and "at home," meaning wherever they want—the house, a café, a park. They move around all the time, and when they do, they meet with whomever they need to as soon as they begin to feel out of touch, which I doubt happens much.

The second error is the assumption that business or the

work environment is the only tribal affiliation people have. By sheer proximity, the workplace tribe may seem to dwarf all the others, but anyone who works at home will find they actually belong to four or five major tribes—starting with the family and extending outward to the neighborhood, the garden club, library volunteers, church, and the like. And, of course, they can meet by the water cooler any time by going into a satellite office for a short while each day, or for several full days in a row.

Working away from the office is an inevitable part of our future. In 1990, only 4 million people telecommuted from home or somewhere else in the United States. By 2000, there were 23.6 million telecommuters. And the work still got done, didn't it?

In the early 1980s, more than two decades, or a tech light-year ago, I was already working three half-days a week at home. Given that summers in Brazil can be sweltering, I was often sitting in shorts by the pool with stacks of yellow telex message forms at my side. In the beginning, I was always skittish when a messenger showed up with the office mail pouch. When the doorbell rang, I would sometimes pull on a pair of trousers, just to look more professional. I kept imagining the young man going back to the company and gossiping that the boss was sunbathing while everyone else was toiling away.

After a while, I figured that everyone already knew I worked at a garden table in my shorts, and I stopped worrying about it. Clearly, I was still getting my work done. Slowly, more of our directors started working from home or elsewhere, then our middle managers, followed by ordinary employees.

In any event, the traditional office will never disappear completely. There will always be a certain percentage of people who cannot work at home because they don't have the space; they have kids in the house, or someone noisily vacuuming; or they don't have the discipline to stop watching TV. For these workers, satellite offices around town are part of the solution.

The decentralized office system has several advantages. Some are obvious. Imagine working five hours after lunch before heading to the parking garage for a sixty-minute drive to a restaurant. You'd arrive at about 7:00 P.M. A Semco worker could leave at 3:00 P.M, drive fifteen minutes to the satellite office closest to the restaurant, read a queue of e-mails, and then saunter slowly to dinner at a quarter to seven. She wouldn't have those e-mails hanging over her head and perhaps might even enjoy a part of a beautiful day before arriving fresh to meet husband and friends.

Another advantage is even more powerful. We've done away with an additional layer of control. If employees can come in any time, work anywhere, and take sole charge of their hours, how can they be controlled? At Semco, managers are concerned with the essence of what employees do for the company, nothing more—certainly not the boarding school issues of who arrived at what time, wearing what clothes, and left when, to go where. So it all comes back to that hardest of all reforms, relinquishing control, and giving it up happily, no less.

Managers who came of age in the many decades since Henry Ford uttered the maxim "You get what you see," want to see their employees at work. But cost and technology mean that even satellite offices will someday be passé. People will work wherever they are. Companies hoping to recruit the best and the brightest must demonstrate that they trust their employees with the freedom to work anywhere. They must assume that they're buying talent and dedication, not what the Brazilians call "butt-on-chair time."

Old-timers can learn a thing or two about this from new-comers. Young workers take to these radical ideas: that they'll have freedom to balance their work and personal lives; that they'll be able to shift around their work and leisure time; and that they can customize their jobs so they remain interested and inspired.

Jose Carlos Reis de Magalhaes was just twenty-three when he came to work at Semco. He was a recent graduate of one of Brazil's top business schools and was working at an important, aggressive investment bank, managing its Internet ventures in the construction industry. An uncle of his introduced us, and I learned to call him by the nickname everyone uses, Zeca. I immediately recognized Zeca's passion for work. He reminded me of myself at his age. Very quickly, I wanted him to help launch Semco Ventures, our high-tech unit. When he quit the investment bank, his infuriated bosses couldn't understand why he left an established, venerable organization for a start-up. But Zeca already felt something the older executives had yet to learn—that status, power, and even money are sometimes not enough to make a job interesting. Or maybe it was just that he wanted to have lunch with his girlfriend occasionally. It's not unusual for Zeca to work twelve-hour days. That makes it hard for him to find time for friends or family. But he regularly has long lunches with his girlfriend. "Only because I work at Semco," he says. "Nowhere else could I do that without feeling guilty."

No one tracks when Zeca puts in his twelve hours, and they're often in the middle of the night. It's up to him. Shortly after he started at Semco, the Brazilian tennis champion Gustavo Kuerten played in the Roland Garros finals—France's Wimbledon—where Kuerten was twice champion. An avid tennis fan, Zeca thought nothing of taking off whole days during the tournament. He didn't philosophize over whether it was right or wrong, and he didn't ask permission. The matches were played in the middle of the day, so Zeca simply made it clear he'd be home watching TV and would work at night instead, maybe. He didn't miss a match, and his work didn't suffer either. On the contrary, pursuing his hobbies or his girlfriend allows him to create balance in his life.

Francisco Alves Pereira is a shop floor manager at Semco Processes, and he likes to stay home on the days before a new project begins. A big man who is rarely without a pair of safety glasses slung around his neck, he prefers to think in comfort and solitude about how he'll set up the factory floor and how to configure space for assembling new machinery. He makes those decisions, instead of an engineer, which is a good example of how democracy blurs the traditional lines between blue- and white-collar workers.

Once Francisco figures out how he wants to assemble a new machine, his team settles on an arrival time. Each project can have a different workday schedule. Usually they choose an early start time to avoid Sao Paulo's horrific traffic jams and to get to and from work earlier than other commuters.

Traffic isn't the only reason for elastic work schedules. If I demand that a worker show up at 8:00 A.M., even if she is someone who regularly sleeps until 9:00, all I will get is a couple of hours of her least productive time. And if I'm closed down at 6:00 P.M., I'm sending her home just as she's hitting her stride. Her biorhythms may dictate that her best hours are from six to eight. Someone else may be alert and prolific after a twenty-minute catnap in the afternoon.

If I insist on standard work hours, I may be sacrificing a certain amount of employee potential every day. By encouraging uniformity, I lose productivity.

By changing the rules, we remove the obstacles that throw people's lives out of whack. When we tell people they're free to work closer to their homes, to come to the office only when they need to, to work odd hours, or to take a weekday off in exchange for work on a Sunday, we're really telling them that there are no rules when it comes to finding a balance in their lives. Everything at Semco that is designed to foster change, innovation, and freedom is really there to help create that balance.

EXHILARATION

On the days that his idol is playing a crucial tennis match, Zeca arrives flushed at the office in the afternoon. We can all see that he's spent the morning screaming and shouting at his television but he doesn't have to be in leisure mode to soar. He's equally turned on by work. People complain that working near him can be distracting because he gets up, walks around excitedly, gestures constantly. When he finally clinches a deal, he's all over the office, beaming and stuttering.

It's just as well that Zeca usually sits next to Jorge Lima, the CEO of our mobile outsourcing unit. At a recent board meeting, Jorge excused himself tersely after receiving a message on his cell phone. We all knew that it concerned a small open bid, with nine contestants, for services at AIG, the insurance giant. He paled immediately, and as he left the room, we commented that he looked like he'd just heard that someone had died. We carried on with our agenda, and then Jorge erupted into the room. Joy radiated from his face. "We won, we won!" he shouted. A smile that shone from ear to ear remained on his face for the rest of the meeting. Far from being spoiled and self-indulgent from enjoying too much workplace freedom, Jorge was free to revel in his, and our, success.

These glittering moments in a career are worth more than any gold watch we could give Zeca or Jorge, or anyone at Semco, and they come from equilibrium.

I, for one, have for decades looked for the balance that leads to happiness. For example, I've always played several musical instruments and felt very connected to music. As a child, I would sit quietly while my mother, a concert-level pianist, played by ear. Her eyesight had been severely affected by eight pregnancies, of which only two succeeded. We shared a love of music.

I spent ten years of my life playing in studios and rock bands, yet I would dearly love to be a symphony conductor. I enjoy the synergy generated when everyone in a group is intent on the same objective.

But even without a symphony to conduct, I often experience life's highs. It happens when my four-year-old son kisses me, or when I read novels by Peter Carey, W.G. Sebald, or Arundhati Roy, when the sun rises at 6:00 A.M. over the fog in the mountains, or when I hear the cello recordings of Pablo Casals. It happens when I feel love intensely, when I write something intriguing, and even when I think I'm onto a new product or service. It hits me when I persuade myself that I've discovered the solution to a problem. Although I'm often wrong, when I'm right the moment of triumph is blissful. These highs are the equivalent of standing on the summit of Mount Everest.

Everyone has lightning flashes of exhilaration, and accumulating a vast and varied collection of these treasures strikes me as a deeply satisfying quest. Imagine a notebook with a tally of moments that made the heart soar, a list that would prove they'd happened, and could, if needed, be shown to everyone as proof that the collector had once defied gravity, dared greatly, heard sweet sounds, and seen much that was true.

Rather than constantly talking about passion—serving

customers passionately, filling in forms passionately—businesses should enable employees to feel exhilaration once in a while. They should let them get involved to the point that they shout "yes!" and give each other high fives because they did it their way, and it worked. People are freed to soar when they find equilibrium between their personal and professional lives, but for most, life is out of whack. Work does not provide fulfillment or exhilaration, and like puppets on a string, they move at someone else's pleasure from nine to five, Monday to Friday and the weekend becomes a whirl of chores and "free time" that offers laughable amounts of genuine leisure or real freedom.

Fortunately, there's another option: Ask why. If exhilaration and balance are absent, why can't they be rediscovered by transforming five days of rat race and two days of enervating "rest" into a seven-day weekend of fulfillment?

The answer is short and sweet.

They can.

Let me show you how we've done it.

- **Why have an office?**

- **Why have employees?**

- **Why have rules?**

THREE

MONDAY

- Try a different job.
- Ramble around.
- Take a nap in a hammock.

YOU'LL KNOW THAT THE seven-day weekend is working its magic when Monday loses its "Oh God, it's Monday!" stigma. It won't happen overnight, but eventually Monday will become just another day of exhilaration.

For that to happen, we must tap into what I call the "reservoir of talent" in the pursuit of personal or company goals. Everyone has a wealth of instincts, interests, and skills that combine to form their talents. Some refer to it as a "calling." Whatever its name, this reservoir can be deeper and more diverse than even the holder himself realizes.

The best way to ensure job satisfaction over the long run is to exhaust that reservoir or to answer the calling. After all, no one works for money alone.

When asked, most workers will tell you there's living, and then there's "making a living." People need more than a paycheck in their lives to feel gratification, yet most cannot figure out how to reconcile living with making a living. A company's goal is to make them one and the same. It would certainly be a happy combination, but only a lucky few can do so. The rest haven't found a way to insert passion into their jobs, and that's why the vast majority of people don't really like what they do all day.

People don't come to work to produce an inferior product, to come late and leave early, to be bored and insubordinate. They work for a reason, for at least some kernel of interest that attracted them to their particular field or profession as a means of earning a paycheck. So why not create an organization that can find out what that is and exploit it.

The first principle to accept is that if an employee has no interest in a product or project, then the venture will never succeed. I'd rather find that out early on, so I can either fire the individual, let him resign or, better yet, move him to another project that does interest him. In traditionally managed companies, this suggests anarchy. As a result, workers are compelled to do jobs they could care less about, and that almost guarantees the company or product will never excel.

I want employees who are excited by their work. If they don't know how to create that passion, I will do my best to help.

Not, however, by simply taking their frustration and wrapping it up in a formulaic step-by-step action plan. Sure, that gives us a road map, but, aside from the highly questionable destination, it also imposes an added burden: I'll have to follow up to make sure they execute the plan. Is there a bigger headache in business than follow-up? "Did you meet your goals this quarter?" "No, I couldn't . . . (plug in an excuse, any excuse)." "But you committed yourself!" How many times a day do people regret the promises they've made, and how much time is wasted by managers fussing and fuming over these broken vows?

I'm not interested in going through the motions, and that's precisely what's happening when you commit yourself to something you really don't want to do. Reluctant warriors don't necessarily go AWOL; however, their stomach for the fight is lacking. That's not to say that people are always thrilled to try something new or difficult, but mature or experienced workers understand that and know once they get involved, they enjoy the challenge and the opportunity for growth.

Here's a counterintuitive idea for you: For a company to excel, employees must be reassured that self-interest, not the company's, is their foremost priority. We believe an employee who puts himself first will be motivated to perform. At Semco this is considered a form of corporate alignment. Without it, a company has to institute programs to pressure, exhort, and compel people to do their jobs. Soon you're roping employees into singing company songs, organizing support teams, and reporting to assemblies for pep talks.

Ever-increasing hours and money are spent on motivational training. Why do people need so much self-help? Instead of signing up for motivation makeovers, they need a different job! You might rotate them to another position, have them work in a different office, ask them to participate more in project meetings, or find another way to work for you on a part-time, commission, or representative basis. We try all of these solutions at Semco, figuring that we can adapt if they can.

What lubricates the process for us is faith—faith supported by experience—that employees can pursue their self-interest and fulfill the company's agenda at the same time. If there's a match or alignment between what we want and what they want, the results will be twofold: While they're busy satisfying themselves, they'll satisfy the company's objectives, too. They succeed, we succeed.

I have another radical notion: It's unfair to expect all employees to feel passionate about their work. Some will, some won't. We must acknowledge that it's human nature to lose interest in anything over time. It's meaningless for traditional companies to boast that they want people with "passion" to work for them, because people cannot be passionate about doing the same thing again and again. That's particularly true for companies that are highly departmentalized, and even more so if the company strictly spells out narrow job parameters. Those are suffocatingly insular organizations; trying to spark passion under such circumstances is deeply frustrating for everyone.

IT'S A DISSERVICE TO EXPECT ALL WORKERS TO FEEL PASSION FOR THEIR JOBS.

Often, firms that make a big deal about passion in employees are really just putting a gloss on a marketing program or, worse, embellishing a mission statement clotted with smarmy phrases. Passion is rare, no wonder it's hard to find in an office job. Expecting all workers to feel passion for their jobs is a cruel disservice because it sets up an unobtainable goal. Let's face it—not every job deserves passion.

The danger in announcing that you expect passion from everybody who works for you is that people weigh their jobs and themselves and conclude that they have no passion, or compare themselves to others and come up short, then give up before they've even started; or turn sour on a job that previously felt okay.

Okay, if employee passion is so hard to come by, but it's a given that you get better work from someone who's interested and invested in a project, what do you do? Companies need to understand that interests tend to be cyclical. At Semco we offer incentives to employees to move around to different jobs and departments. It's another avenue for them to dip into their reservoir of talent and develop independence. If they're moving around following an inner radar, then they won't rely on the company to tell them what to do. Instead of feigning passion or fretting at the lack thereof, this inner radar will keep them beamed into one of my favorite compound words—self-interest.

A great deal of employee satisfaction occurs when individuals have some leverage over the logistics of their job. At Semco we don't dictate to people what their responsibilities are; we assume that as adults they can figure out for themselves what it takes to do their job, and that without guidelines to adhere to, they're more likely to test the boundaries of what they do. That testing often leads to new business practices or new ventures for the company and new challenges for employees.

Without a formal job description, people can wander into neighboring work activities without being chased away for trespassing. Semco has a slew of assistants, junior personnel, and others who regularly meander among tasks and projects. It's unclear where they officially belong. The answer, of course, is nowhere specific, and that's fine because they work without a confining checklist of tasks or responsibilities; they have the freedom to decide for themselves what their job entails. They self-manage. They also control where they work, when they work, and how much they are paid for their work. This may seem haphazard, but it's one of our many solutions to the limitations of traditional workplace arrangements. The status quo simply isn't good enough.

Unfortunately, our society conditions us to accept boredom from an early age. We're taught to expect it in school. I believe that employees deserve the latitude to try different jobs because many of them emerge from an education system that compels them to make career and training choices at a very young age, when they have little information about professions and no experience.

Some people reject a future of conventional jobs to become painters and writers, taking their reservoir of talent with them. Those who stick around simply learn to live with boredom without drawing on their true talents, which is a huge waste of human potential. So if Semco didn't allow rambling, we couldn't get the best out of our people. We compensate for society's conditioning by letting people ramble around the company and explore their own interests. As a consequence, the company rambles with them into opportunities and new businesses.

Auro Alves is a sales and technical-assistance manager at Semco, but he began his career with us as a truck driver. He'd driven a bus in Sao Paulo before joining Semco and expected that he'd spend his life as a heavy-duty commercial driver. Less than five months after coming to Semco, he moved into product acquisition, and eight months after that, took a job as a junior buyer. He got involved in union activities, discovered that he liked being a leader, and that other workers were comfortable with his management style, too. He had a knack for coming up with new ways of doing old tasks at Semco in order to involve more people.

While at Semco, Auro has taken dozens of elective courses, including English, Spanish, computers, negotiation technique, sales methods, and customer care. He's had offers to work elsewhere, but turned them down because Semco allows him to grow. Auro isn't finished exploiting his own "reservoir of talent." He has a five-year plan of his own, even if the company frowns on them for itself. He owns a beach house in Peruibe and spends part of his seven-day weekend there fishing and getting to know the local people. He plans to move there one day and run his own "virtual business" as a supplier or consultant to Semco.

Job rotation exposes workers like Auro to different challenges. Also when people change jobs, they're forced to work in a new environment and sometimes even cross over to another tribe. Moving around limits tribal affiliations that are detrimental to democracy, communication, and innovation.

Another element of job satisfaction is stress, and stress levels are highest where balance is lowest. It often reflects the difference between expectation and reality. If an organization sets expectations too high and then fails to meet them, employee stress levels will obviously skyrocket. The carefully cultivated balance between individual aspirations and company goals will be upset. That's less likely to happen if people can set their

WORKPLACE STRESS REFLECTS THE DIFFERENCE BETWEEN EXPECTATION AND REALITY.

own expectations for themselves and for the company. Even so, at times stress is inevitable, and seven-day-week-style activities, such as golf before a conference call, or a break on the beach between inventories, help reduce it to reasonable levels. Executives who are embarrassed to take these breaks or companies that frown on them are shortsighted. Stress is a major disruption; and its effects, such as burnout, are grim reapers for talented people.

I spent many years dealing with everyday stress by setting my watch five minutes fast. I thought that was really smart. I'd increase my chances of being on time and also give myself a little boost of relief at the last minute when I realized I had five minutes to spare. I know people who started out innocently enough, like me, and now set their watches fifteen or twenty minutes ahead.

Luckily, I've come to my senses. I gave a talk recently at Semco called "The Merits of Omission." I recommended that everyone set back their watches. It works like this:

Since this chapter focuses on Monday, suppose you're stuck in a Monday morning traffic jam on the way to an appointment. You could have scheduled the get-together for Saturday, and you're kicking yourself for not doing it since now you've got gridlock, horns, and lights that go from red to green to red before you can inch ahead. Soon you're ready to punch numbers into your cell phone to let people know you're going to be late. However thoughtful, it doesn't change the fact that several people are waiting for you to arrive.

Some fixed variables are at work here. First, you may be one of those people who are always in a rush, always late. I used to be chronically tardy, a bad habit that worsened when I moved close to our head office ten years ago. I was only one traffic light away, too close to require me to leave earlier as a precaution against delays and, as a result, I never arrived on time. I was constantly rushing into the office out of breath, long after the people who lived across town were already seated.

Peter Kuhlman, an executive at RGIS, recalls one of my explanations for a missed meeting. I was waylaid at home, I said, waiting for a physical therapist to treat a back problem. The man never arrived, and I found out later that he'd gone to the wrong house and given a massage to the wrong patient. Peter, of course, considered this the lamest excuse he had ever heard. In truth, my neighbor's name is also Ricardo, and my street number is 304, and his 204, and someone in his house was changing massage therapists at the time. But I concede that this is a long shot.

Another fixed variable is that once late, and despite your fuming as another car cuts in front of you, there is very little you can do about it. Sure, you can kick yourself every four minutes for not having left earlier, or you can also think up wilder and wilder excuses, but traffic alibis no longer impress anyone. For years, I thought Sao Paulo led the world in traffic snarls until I experienced Bangkok gridlock. It took me an hour and twenty minutes to drive to an early meeting just ten blocks from my hotel. I asked what time I should plan to set out for the airport that night, and was told to leave immediately.

That's just a form of modern life stress, but it needn't be. Imagine the same situation with your watch set back fifteen minutes. Now, you are sitting in the same mess, glancing at your watch on occasion, relieved there's still time left. The delays are the same, your reaction is the same, but now you're surprised to see that you're late when you pass the clock above the secretary's desk. Even better, you may never find out because your hosts are gentlemanly and don't mention it. No stress, voilà!

You may accuse me of being cavalier about making other people wait, but I'm very rarely late any more. Punctuality is a mind-set that's cultivated by the seven-day weekend. It really has no relation to watches. There are always plenty of clocks around, or people with watches to consult. I stand by my point that stress is the difference between your expectations and reality. You feel stress because of something left undone or a place not reached. With a seven-day weekend you feel there's time to do what needs to be done and to get to where you need to be.

Stress can affect anyone at any time.

Suppose you are a forty-one-year-old woman who cannot get pregnant. Stress. You are a five-year-old who left his knapsack home. Stress. You have 152 pages to copy and another customer is waiting on the other side of the copy machine. Stress. You wave at your neighbor in the suburbs every day, and his company Lexus reminds you that he's two management echelons above you and four years younger. Stress. You rush through the house because you can smell the pie burning in the

> **YOU DON'T HAVE TO LIKE THE PEOPLE YOU WORK WITH. RESPECT FOR THEIR PERFORMANCE IS ENOUGH.**

oven, and knock a bottle of red wine onto the white carpet. Stress.

Even going on vacation becomes stressful because of the many things that need to be arranged before you leave. Not to mention the stress when you are about to return and start to fret over the work or mail or errands awaiting you. No wonder there is so much shouting at airport counters.

Lack of information adds to stress, too. When you feel some strange pain in your stomach, or cannot see well through your left eye, nothing relieves your stress like the doctor telling you that it's just a virus going around.

Another source of stress and disappointment is the expectation that the workplace is an extended family. People want their jobs to provide a sense of belonging, to feel they're taken care of, to bond with colleagues. But they're looking for things the company can't supply. They should keep the company role in perspective. The first expectation to kill is that big families are fun and supportive. Romantic, but untrue. Anyone with a big family can tell you there are always people they don't like among their own relatives. Yet large numbers of family-owned and midsize businesses foster this notion. They do this because the image of "family" projects an image of loyalty, mutual support, and shared culture.

The fact is, you don't have to like people to work with them, and finding compatibility of purpose at work does not require surrounding yourself only with those you like. You can admire people, even if you don't like them. There are several managers at Semco that I would never have lunch with—I don't empathize with them at all—some I downright dislike. But that is irrelevant, because I still respect their style and performance.

The stress-free workplace that is most productive is the one where workers respect each other's differences.

THE ART OF FLEX ABILITY

Semco is experimenting with various approaches, but we're still evolving techniques to return control to our people over a very important piece of real estate—their destiny. One is a plan called "Up 'n' Down Pay," where employees flexibly manage their pay. The idea is that certain periods in people's lives are very different, and that enabling them to adapt their pay and work hours accordingly will pay dividends. Employees would look to balance the company's present needs with their own and adjust the pay package accordingly.

If someone is going through a phase in which they would rather work less and lower their pay accordingly, the company would do its best to adapt. A mother who wants more time for her children would turn to a committee for help in locating another person who would gladly take over 30 percent of her job responsibilities, assuming that the person's business unit cannot do without 100 percent of her time. The committee would have a database of candidates to fill our constant demand for part-time work, or it could turn to the full three thousand employees and appeal to anyone interested in switching jobs or sharing tasks. This flexibility would make it possible for people with temporary interests, problems, illnesses, or family issues to scale back or freshen their minds, knowing that they are not in danger of derailing their career.

We don't come up with these ideas in a vacuum. They're prompted by the end of the Monday-to-Friday workweek and by the fact that like it or not, we're facing a new world of multiple careers for most professionals. This dovetails nicely with our new retirement concept.

By most standards, Semco's Retire-a-Little program sounds crazy. But it takes life cycles into account like this: By plotting the curve of human health, you easily see that the peak of physical capability is in one's twenties and thirties. The downturn is usually steepest and deepest after the age of sixty. On another graph, you can plot financial independence and see that the zenith usually occurs between age fifty and sixty. On a third graph, idle time naturally peaks after seventy. In other words, the time and money lines are up when the health line is down for older workers, and the opposite is true for younger people.

The sad conclusion is that when you're most fit to realize your dreams, you don't have the money or leisure time for them, and when you have the most time and money on hand, you no longer have the physical stamina. Shouldn't this system be replaced with one that allows employees to redraw those lines to square the life cycle with a career cycle? Let's shift some of the strengths of youth to the days of old age, and vice versa, and use the business organization to do it.

With our Retire-a-Little program, you acquire from the company as much early retirement time as you wish. For example, 10 percent of your time, which amounts to an afternoon per week, and the company sells it to you at a discount slightly below par value by reducing your take home pay by a small amount. Now, Wednesday afternoons are yours to pursue those interests that you would ordinarily reserve for retirement: fishing, weaving, gardening, studying. The company's amount of payroll is reduced a bit and so is your paycheck, but you've authentically and unarguably bought back some freedom from the boss.

Semco adds yet another dimension. You receive a voucher for work after your retirement. So if you took off a hundred Wednesday afternoons, you are now entitled to redeem the vouchers after your retirement by showing up with them and saying, "I'd now like to redeem my vouchers to work one Wednesday a week for two years and receive proportional pay."

You've effectively exchanged early retirement for later work. This year, you rock climb on Wednesdays. Ten years from now on Wednesday afternoons you think about our new product.

It's too early to know how we'll deal with the offshoot issues that this program may raise; whether the company will still exist when they retire, whether too many people show up for work that we no longer have. I can think of many reasons to hesitate, as I could have for every one of the thirty or so innovative ideas we have put in place in the last two decades. Nevertheless, like everything else at Semco, Retire-a-Little is chiefly designed to push boundaries and test the future today.

Another plan, called Work 'n' Stop, complements the first two. It gives employees up to three years to take off for whatever purpose they want. A committee acts like an internal headhunter to search for replacements for those who are seeking sabbaticals. If someone within Semco agrees to take the job on a temporary basis, the employee who wants a break would be fairly certain he could return. If the headhunters must go outside the company to fill the post, returning and reclaiming the old job is more problematic but not out of the question. At any rate there's usually an interesting open slot somewhere, and our employees love the chance to ramble.

To finance these sabbaticals, Semco allows employees to earmark and set aside a monthly portion of their pay. The company acts as banker by keeping the money but releases it whenever the employee has enough to underwrite his time off and wants to make a withdrawal. The company might even retain 30 percent until the person returns to work. For the employee, it'd be a golden opportunity to self-manage, to balance work and personal life. For the company, it'd be an incentive to break with routine. The amount put aside by the company, would be a worthwhile investment for employees, who would come back refreshed and invigorated by the outside world. It would pay for itself in productivity and longevity, not to mention the decrease in turnover. After all, according to a study from the University of Pennsylvania, it costs companies between $22,000 and $45,000 to fully train an average new employee. The money set aside for this program would total far less. It would pay people a safety-net income while they pursue their dreams, and would certainly reduce turnover.

These ideas could be expanded to training, too. A company would set aside a sum every year for each employee's training. Companies already allocate 1 to 3 percent of their revenue for this, but they leave it up to HR to distribute the money.

But since we're talking about self-directed careers, people would take their allocation, which would be different per person according to the job held, and "buy" training from the company menu. In this manner, the company would extract itself from the paternalistic position of planning people's careers for them.

If someone is an airport check-in agent, for example, and the company feels that fifty hours of classroom time is necessary for that job, they'll designate that. But it will be up to that agent to take those classes or not. They could apply the allocation toward management training or foreign language classes instead of traffic control or customer relations, subjects the company might otherwise prefer. Rather than disallowing that, the company acquiesces with the proviso that the employee skillfully handle traffic or customers without taking classes in those areas.

Wait a minute, you're saying, how does this ensure a well-trained employee? The proof is in the performance. In our system at Semco, where people only survive by performing, that same check-in counter employee would be responsible for making things happen. For example, if he or she learns quickly on the job, those fifty classroom hours of mandatory, one-size-fits-all training would have been a waste. However, time spent learning a language, computer skills, or baggage handling—whatever the employee is drawn to—may be much more valuable to the company. The proof, as to whether it was a wise allocation of training time, rests with how well the employee ultimately does the job.

Again, all it takes is confidence that employees are responsible adults, not ignorant newcomers who know next to nothing about what their jobs require. This system would also reveal an individual's real interests, which in turn could make business far more efficient.

These concepts should also apply to benefits. Flexible benefits are just becoming an option for some workers. But more creativity is needed to take benefits to their natural end in organizations looking for self-determination and self-management. Employees should be able to customize their health plans, pension fund contributions, insurance, meal tickets, and even health club or collective purchasing programs.

By letting the employees make their own calculations and freely choose their own health benefits, we transfer responsibility to our people. We hand them their freedom.

We always hope that on their own, people will discover their true calling. Of course it doesn't always happen. Sometimes the person who only aspires to a dignified, nine-to-five job and enough money to make ends meet, offers us a mutually beneficial arrangement. Sometimes we have a boring job that needs to be done. Work is a noble undertaking for a doctor with an ideal, a fireman with courage, a mailman with stamina, a businessman with ideas or excess energy. But there are also people who work in the doctor's office, or in the administrative department of the fire department or mail system, and on assembly lines. Most of them are not answering a calling.

Those people constitute the vast majority of workers in the world. That isn't to say that a factory worker, a bank clerk, or a shop assistant cannot be happy at work, but the chance is slim that they are exhausting their reservoir of talent. It's my theory that the slow and measured use of that reserve is what makes life worthwhile.

Scuba diving offers a good analogy. You are given approximately one hour's worth of air in your scuba tank and want to remain submerged as long as possible to swim, roam, and marvel. If, perchance, you get stuck in a cave, it's always helpful to have a little bit of air left in the tank. Therefore, planning a forty-five-minute dive would be wise. Yet there are people who resurface in half that time with an empty tank. They breathed too hard and too fast. They had a reservoir but used it up too quickly—and missed out on seeing the rest of what the ocean had to offer.

On land, each of us has a life's worth of air. We can consume it quickly and then fret about all the things we didn't have time to do, or we can pace ourselves.

Too many people never learn this. They lack balance between work and personal life, and before they know it their opportunities are gone too. Receiving a gold watch after thirty years at an automobile manufacturer is dreary compensation indeed. In contrast, there are people who make their jobs coincide with their calling, no matter what.

Clovis Bojikian, Semco's Human Resources icon, is one such case. His first job at Semco was as our Human Resources director, back when we still had such a position. We decided the department really had no reason to exist. The first Human Resources departments date to the turn of the century and blossomed because managers were uncomfortable dealing with personnel issues. Over time, it became accepted that managers couldn't recruit, train, place ads, hire headhunters, do career plans or employee reviews, and serve as an objective third party.

Yet these are some of the most important issues a manager faces. We decided that Semco couldn't operate that way, that whatever problems managers had dealing with personnel issues had to be solved at the source. We retained two people in HR, Clovis and his colleague, Flor, to be our eyes and ears to the outside world on the subject. They have become technical experts, and they advise our managers.

Although he's technically an HR person, Semco's unique corporate structure allows for people to pursue what inspires them, and Clovis has proven often inspired. Clovis has an affinity for blue-collar employees, and has always said he could do more for them than for office workers. As Semco grew, our offices became fancier and employee facilities improved. We never made a deliberate distinction between white- and blue-collar workers, but humans tend to be tribal, and because of that, blue-collar workers from the factory floor just didn't hang around drinking coffee in the staff lounge. As the offices expanded and were updated, the factory remained the same.

All of which fueled Clovis's dream of a rest space for the shop workers in the garden outside the factory. He was always occupied with other tasks, so it took years to get around to it. But finally, a one-thousand-square-foot area was set aside, an architect was hired, and sketches were produced. They included a kiosk with a barbecue area, a coffee machine, and a refrigerator. The garden had benches and shaded rest areas.

When I saw the sketches, I remembered an old dream of mine of hanging hammocks for worker catnaps. The body's natural biorhythms make an afternoon nap almost essential, yet modern societies have done away with the practice of the siesta, though Brazil, like the United States and the United Kingdom, never adopted them. Even though medical science has long recognized that afternoon naps are natural, Western culture has mocked and derided the need to sleep during the day as a sign of laziness and lack of discipline. The National Sleep Foundation in the United States says only 15 percent of workers are allowed to doze on the job, even though the vast majority of people get less than the eight hours of sleep most of us need.

A month and $30,000 later, the entire garden, with hammocks, was ready. It has been used prodigiously since. The garden slowly brought people around to reconsidering their productive moments, their need for silence, and the need to recharge their batteries. Now there are people there most of the day.

Another reform that occurred on Clovis's watch was the advent of flextime, which came about after a conversation he had with a shipping and receiving clerk named Antonio Santos, who mentioned that he had never been able to pick up his kids from school when they were growing up because of his work schedule. With Clovis's encouragement, Antonio's group decided to start work well before morning rush hour to avoid traffic. In return, they left for home much earlier. Antonio was ecstatic because, for the first time in his life, he could pick up his granddaughter from school. He was more moved by the unexpected freedom to be at the school, waiting for his granddaughter, than he was about beating rush hour.

Antonio's joy over the workers' garden is better than money to Clovis.

Shortly after his return, the dramatic changes that we were making at Semco caught the attention of Brazil's media. Journalists who discovered Semco also discovered Clovis, and the magazine and newspaper articles were followed by many attempts to poach him. Debt-free, Clovis refused these offers without considering them, even one to become HR director at the biggest media corporation in Brazil with a salary three times as large. There was another from the biggest services group in Brazil at double his salary. He was unimpressed, and instead stayed at Semco without seeking a raise, and without even mentioning the offers until months later. Clovis knew our numbers. It was clear to him that we couldn't pay him more. Besides, he was earning something much more valuable than money.

"At Semco I was living the most exciting time of my career," Clovis recalls. "The changes we were proposing were revolutionary. Our shop-floor workers were participating in company policy and decisions at a level never seen before. I felt honored by the other offers, but I didn't even consider leaving." Having the power to improve people's lives was worth more than a triple-fold raise at another company. There's a word for that—"calling."

ALTERNATIVE RECRUITING

Traditional companies recruit and hire for openings within the organization that are usually described in a detailed job outline and accompanied by a list of academic and career prerequisites. Their first priority is filling those requirements. At Semco, our focus is on hiring people who want to work for us because there's a "click" between their life purpose and the company's business purpose. We have been known to place ads that say, "We have no openings, but apply anyway. Come in and talk about what you might do for us, and how we might create a position for you."

We're always looking for alternative ways to bring people into the company and to connect their callings and talents with our needs. This started at a time when Semco needed new blood but couldn't afford to increase the payroll. The first ad made it plain that there were no openings, but we offered to show interested people around the company for a day and then accept proposals for a way to work with us; i.e., for a fee, a commission, through subcontracting, percentages, by the job, whatever might work. Hundreds of people visited our factories and offices over a two-day period. We accepted proposals of work from thirty-five people and eventually hired two of them.

One of the proposals to overhaul our machinery to operate more efficiently came from a man with decades of experience in machine maintenance. He suggested a "success fee," or a percentage of the money we saved in operating costs. His work demonstrated the wisdom of outsourcing, and it was so successful that it was ultimately applied to other parts of our engineering areas. Project design, planning, drafting, and machinery maintenance were all eventually outsourced.

Why is it that church groups, amateur choirs, or chess teams have such a high degree of commitment, but companies have to train, retrain, motivate, and remotivate all year round—just to keep people from biting off customers' heads over the phone? And why do those same bored or bitter phone attendants leave the office fed up with their workday only to transform into joyful choir singers that same evening?

Could it be that "calling" is difficult to reconcile with office or factory jobs? Do nine-to-five jobs somehow naturally attract people who have no calling? Is the majority of humanity stuck doing jobs that are unfulfilling?

Is it perhaps unrealistic to expect that modern production methods be compatible with excitement? Are we just kidding ourselves when we hope that all of our employees will jump from their beds on Monday morning, excited with what awaits them at the job? Do we just train them enough to do what needs to be done, and reawaken them from their boredom every so often with tricks, campaigns and subtle threats?

I'm always skeptical of companies that search for "passion" in their employees, who portray their workforce as a happy, smiling family that cannot wait for you to bring your needs or problems to their doorstep.

The truth is closer to this: Most of the people who look for common office or factory jobs do not have a calling for what the work entails. They just need a job, to keep themselves and their family thriving so they can pursue their real calling. Is it a waste of time to deal with these people? Hardly, since they still have a reservoir of talent worth discovering. They just need the opportunity to discover it themselves. The discovery process is of great value to the individual and the organization.

"Discovery" is one of those splendid words that radiates power, like balance and exhilaration, passion and calling, satisfaction and fulfillment. The antithesis is control. A mean and confining word, control offers the illusion—delusion—of security and order. "Take control. Be in control. Control the play." A word suited to jailers. And I'm no jailer. When my control means your captivity, I'd prefer to take an exhilarating plunge into a reservoir of talent no matter how uncertain. The hell with control. The hell with "Oh, God, it's Monday." I say TGIM: Thank God, it's Monday—another day of exhilaration, another day of discovery.

■ **Why do the same job year after year?**

■ **Why not retire at age forty, go back to work at sixty ?**

■ **Why wear a wrist watch?**

FOUR

TUESDAY

- Make friends with a new customer.
- Get lost in space.
- Study the company's balance sheet.

TUESDAY IS THE GREAT dead zone of the conventional work-week. It's neither beginning nor middle, and it's uncomfortably far from the end. But in the seven-day weekend scheme of things, Tuesday is ideal for thinking about why we do what we do. And ultimately, the answer is: to make the life trip worthwhile and to feel alive with purpose.

For work to be personally meaningful, it has to be customized to people's talents. That may sound obvious, but it's more than matching a résumé to a job description. A good illustration of the point is Jorge Lima's genius for pursuing customers.

Jorge once spent an entire week riding the elevators in a financial institution in hopes of running into a reclusive and recalcitrant director. He knew that if he could meet the man, his talents for friendship and persuasion would rule the day. Jorge was running an operation for the institution, he needed more freedom, and the director wasn't being cooperative. So Jorge took to riding the elevator up and down, knowing that eventually his quarry would get on. On one of those vertical voyages from heaven to hell and back, in which he counted seventeen round-trips, the director finally stepped into the elevator. Jorge struck up a conversation, and got what he needed. They are personal friends to this day. This talent for ferreting out a target is rare, and sometimes it even leads to trouble.

One of Jorge's targets was a very difficult potential customer. This senior bank executive was humorless, curt, aggressive, abrasive; and he was universally feared within the bank. Jorge had tried to contact him on a cold call in the hopes of offering this man our services. After many failed attempts, Jorge learned that a mutual friend provided armored car services to this banker's department, and the friend arranged for a meeting.

The friend advised Jorge to be quick and to the point and to refrain from his usual smiling, warm conversation, any physical contact, or instant intimacy.

Jorge arrived, was kept waiting, and was finally let in to see this man, who barely raised his eyes. Jorge's interpersonal skills and his invitation to lunch extended the fifteen-minute interview. At the restaurant, both men had a beer, and the banker loosened up. Soon they were talking about how some men needed to hang "bimbos" on their arms.

They laughed as they pointed to some overdressed women decked out in Versace creations. Jorge then guffawed and beat his thighs as the most extravagant of the women walked in. "That," he exclaimed, "is the queen of all bimbos!" He roared with laughter as the banker got up and went over to the woman, presumably to play along and say something funny to her. Instead he brought her to the table, and Jorge's heart sank as the bank director introduced her as his wife, Cristina.

Jorge excused himself, went to the men's room, threw cold water on his face, and called his wife on his cell phone to ask her what he should do. She advised him to go back and pretend nothing had happened, which he did. In the end, he got the contract.

In spite of this pratfall, I think it's safe to say that when Jorge can use his schmoozing talent, it makes him feel alive with purpose. But talent, or the obsession that comes with a particular talent, is not the same as doing something exceptional, despite the widespread belief that this is so. There are talents that few of us imagine possessing. I don't mean playing the violin like a world-class musician. I mean the ability to stay awake, night after night, in the dark and silence, watching a blue-tinged monitor in a night watchman's cabin. Or being an orderly in a public hospital in the developing world, cleaning latrines, making beds for the sick. These are talents of great importance to all of us.

I realize that many people who fill these jobs have no option, that someone has to do the work. But among the countless people who work simply to earn a living, there are many that find a niche for themselves. Plenty of jobs are full of tasks that don't require talent, but to do them well, skills are necessary; and talent doesn't hurt.

When my father arrived in Brazil from Austria in the early 1950s, he started his company from a kitchen table in a downtown apartment. The very first employee he hired was Roberval Couto. Roberval was with Semco until he retired. He drove our American visitors to and from the airport, and although he spoke no English, he had painstakingly learned to tell one and all that he had picked up my birth certificate when I was born in 1959.

The interesting thing about Roberval was that he started as a messenger or an "office boy," according to the politically incorrect term of the time. After thirty-five years and many opportunities, he had become, lo and behold, an office boy. And that's how he retired. But anyone would be hard put to find a happier person or one who matched Roberval's ample smile, springy step, and waving hand. He would proudly tell me how he could deliver a letter quicker by ducking under a parking garage, bypassing traffic through side streets, or taking the service elevator from the mezzanine floor; and he'd giggle at the thought of the other messengers waiting in line.

Roberval had skills and a talent both for what he did and for being happy. The two merged within him, and there is no greater talent indeed. Every time we tried to augment his income or promote him, he would laugh and say, "Oh, no, you won't catch me being an office clerk. Excuse me, I've got to run." We simpletons thought that sticking him behind a desk would improve his life and chances for success. Meanwhile, he taught us the meaning of success.

Few are as fulfilled and satisfied with their jobs as Roberval, which explains why companies campaign so relentlessly to motivate employees. Maybe they wouldn't have to campaign so hard if they made an effort to talk to their employees, find out what they wanted to accomplish, and then gave them the freedom to pursue their ideas. But that rarely happens.

And yet, managers don't think it unreasonable to expect someone to maintain their level of interest and activity for many years.

The result, of course, is that people have no incentive to veer from the proverbial nine-to-five job attitude. Unfortunately that attitude, which means they'll follow their job description to the letter but not one bit more, can cripple a company.

LABOR UNREST

For decades, unions have striven to change working conditions, building solidarity among workers and harnessing collective indignation over the poor terms imposed by big business. It was Henry Ford who said, "Why is it that every time I ask for a pair of hands, a brain comes attached?"

During the long, bitter winter strikes at the Midwest vehicle and heavy equipment manufacturers in the mid-1980s, International Harvester, Caterpillar, and the Big Three automakers were besieged by workers on picket lines marching back and forth in the cold, day after day, sometimes for months on end. They weren't stomping through the snow just for extra money and benefits.

I calculated the impact of the raises that workers were demanding during one of those particularly prolonged strikes, and compared them to what management was willing to cede. The net difference was 1.8 percent. To the company, this meant tens of millions of dollars a year. To the worker, it was the price of a small television set, and no one would walk a picket line in the freezing cold for three months for such a paltry prize. Worker dissatisfaction and frustration are usually caused by indignation at not being heard. Money isn't the real issue.

Some of the bitterness was also created by draconian labor policies. Jacques Nasser, former CEO of Ford, had to carry out his company's policy of firing 5 to 10 percent of the poorest performing employees, which didn't help create goodwill with the workforce. It's a philosophy that mirrors the bell-curve grading scheme at business schools, where it's considered a given that 10 percent of your managers and employees are subpar, and must be pruned like dead wood for the good of the company.

Even from a purely financial point of view, it is far wiser to pinpoint the problem that's causing the poor performance and to solve it instead of wasting the time, effort, and money already invested in the employee. It's idiotic to blindly repeat that investment on a new worker, and run the risk that the next person may turn out to be an underperformer as well, particularly if his or her morale is destroyed by an us-versus-them mentality that, I believe, incited those crippling strikes in the 1980s.

The decline of unions has been celebrated by industry captains, much as the fall of the Berlin Wall apparently vindicated free-market politicians. But these stories are far from over. Unions have been largely broken by the unemployment that came from globalization. Much of the pressure that used to come from them has been transferred to nongovernmental organizations (NGOs). In Naples or Seattle, being dragged off picket lines or Greenpeace stunts, boycotting a company for child labor or discrimination, NGO cadres that favor direct and in some cases violent action have taken up the voice of the worker.

What is the twenty-first-century format of dialogue and negotiation with workers? We at Semco are experimenting with one, considering that we don't believe that broken unions have done away with the need for power sharing with employees. Our employees have elected 117 trustees (one for every group, location, or site) who are empowered to represent the people of Semco, and defend its "constitution." Our constitution is of course not written; it just conceptually encompasses the basic values and culture that are currently in place (and that change with time).

The trustees take turns on the twelve-member board of

trustees that meets monthly and addresses practices by management that may be at odds with the current values of Semco as a whole. Two of these board of trustees members have a seat and vote on Semco's board of directors, and an agenda time allotment to bring up and negotiate whatever they find necessary.

No one knows where this will lead, and what power sharing or cohabitation it will carve, but it will certainly bring us face-to-face with our own inconsistencies, and give our employees a chance to feel effectively empowered—with a strong voice. We should never be scared of our own people, whatever it is they have to say or demand—the result is always vastly superior to the ostrich approach of looking for subtle ways of keeping their demands subdued.

A company's employees are not the enemy. They are valuable assets and worth investing in. Lucia Kobayashi is a good example. A daughter of Japanese immigrants, Lucia is a funny, optimistic woman whose blue hair makes it easy to pick her out of a crowd. She chose a career in marketing, joined Semco during the infamous dot-com era, and failed to produce as much as expected, so her contract wasn't renewed.

Since we believe in giving people time and opportunity to prove themselves, another unit launching new software for construction companies hired unlucky Lucia. Unlucky because that ill-fated project became known as "the Kursk," after the Russian submarine that tragically sank with all hands aboard. When our Kursk went to the bottom, Lucia was then hired to provide marketing to new ventures.

After a few months, that group realized that Lucia was not

right for them, either. They didn't renew her contract. Yet we still didn't want to let her go. Her managers felt she just had to find the right spot, so they put out the word she was available.

Then I hired her. Even unluckier for Lucia. I can be quite a pain in the behind when I want something exactly as I want it. There was an infamous business trip to Rio where I wanted to visit two hotels, even though one was open only from Thursday to Saturday, while the other had conventions during the week. I wanted to meet the owner of one, who was there only on Saturdays, and have lunch at the other hotel on Sunday. I insisted on using the airport nearest the second hotel, but I needed a car that was only available at the airport closest to the first. Lucia gave up, more or less fired me, and decided to move to Japan.

Before she could do that, however, another Semco unit that sells software offered her a marketing job, and she's been there since, doing nicely. She might retire at the company, and might still move around until she finds something that even better suits her blue-hair style. She's been in the bottom 10 percent several times already, and would have been thrown out by the Fords and GEs of this world long ago.

ECOLOGY IN BALANCE

Organizations rarely believe they're to blame when an employee underperforms, but if the organization doesn't provide the opportunity for success, it's their fault when people falter. At Semco we accept that every individual wants and needs a

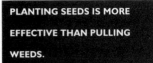

PLANTING SEEDS IS MORE EFFECTIVE THAN PULLING WEEDS.

worthwhile pursuit in life. It's up to us to provide the environment and opportunity for their gratification.

We resort to a series of programs and practices like job rotation, reverse evaluation, and self-management. They're intended to help people tap their reservoir of talent and to preclude the need for weeding out. We never assume there are weeds among us.

As with any microenvironment, our ecology has to be balanced. Compare it to Mao Tse-tung's war against disease-carrying pigeons. The snakes deployed to control the pigeon population were wildly successful and left the Chinese with a huge snake problem.

It's the same with people. Purging dead wood inevitably creates another predicament. People soon find themselves working in a reign of terror, their creativity and conscientiousness smothered by fear. It prevents an organization from learning from its mistakes. Process is paramount to knowledge, and mistakes are powerful catalysts for the process.

Former GE CEO Jack Welch was once asked by the manager of a small Manhattan men's clothing store whether he should adopt Welch's practice of firing the bottom 10 percent of his sales staff each year. The man employed twenty people, but Jack assured him that it was the right thing to do. I disagree. Many hard-nosed executives, who always see the marketplace as a walk on the wild side, preach the gospel of survival of the fittest, but they're really just using fear as a management technique. It spawns a regime of microterror and veiled threats where managers tell employees to stay busy and keep your numbers up or we'll have your ass. As far as I'm concerned you'll get bigger numbers—sustainable numbers—by nurturing employees. Today's problem child can be tomorrow's superstar.

Anyone who has been through an MBA program knows how Welch-style Darwinism works. At the end of the first year, the underperformers are dismissed from the program. Shy and thoughtful students are at an automatic disadvantage, since evaluation normally includes air time, the graduate business school practice whereby MBA students are rated according to how often they wave their hands in the air to speak out in class. However well these mild-mannered intellects do on the tests, lack of air time unfairly implies that they are not suited to the rough-and-tumble world of big business. On the contrary, they may be brilliantly equipped to quietly outmaneuver a bombastic opponent, yet as a result of the air time yardstick, they may lose out to peers who tend to be openly aggressive, individualistic, and terror-tested, yet underexposed to teamwork, ego control, soft tactics, and compromise. When the corporate behemoths park their scouts outside ivy-covered brick walls, the tough-minded students within are already well steeled for the relentless career drive that awaits them.

This is too bad for the graduates and the companies that recruit them. Very few new MBA graduates can accurately assess which organization that approaches them with a job offer will meet their long-term need to breathe slowly from their talent oxygen tanks, so they can take in the scenery along the way, which puts them at risk of burning out too fast. And by only targeting the type As that the MBA programs churn out, the employers are missing some extraordinary talent that could make all the difference to their success and profitability.

I once knew a Brazilian who was graduating from Harvard Business School. His living room featured a large wall chart with vertical and horizontal grids detailing the fourteen job offers he was considering. The chart was rich with information like salary and benefits, insurance, geographical location, company statistics—a scoreboard of his success.

It was also absurd. Not only had he reduced his opportunities to a jumble of numbers, he also assumed that his decision would be based on a complex mathematical model. The chart left out the most important consideration, his calling, and the chance that one of the jobs above all others would let him maximize his talents and satisfy his identity.

In the end, my Brazilian friend took a job with one multinational company only to see it merge with another company four months later. He was sent to another country in another job but left the business two years later. Today he's working for his fourth company, exactly when he calculated he would be in this stage of his career in the first, defunct corporation. So much for statistical charts. He's still chasing an elusive idea about the perfect job, framing it all around his MBA and technical background, while the air in his tank is seeping uselessly away.

Those narrow-minded corporate scouts would never understand how I could consider a cleaning lady to be as valuable to Semco as our top executives. But I do. Why? Because when the late Rogerio Ottolia, who at the time was CEO of our digital scale factory, asked her exactly what her job was, without missing a beat, she replied, "I build scales."

This is what I mean when I say that talent can be found at every level in your organization. This woman knew her work contributed more to Semco than just her efforts with a broom, a bucket, and a pushcart. She didn't feel pigeonholed, labeled, or compelled to stick to an anonymous job description. She identified with the reason our scale factory exists. Maybe one of her suggestions will save Semco money or spark an idea for a new product.

That's not so far-fetched when you realize that, like everyone at Semco, the cleaning staff takes part in a monthly meeting that analyzes the company numbers. There they learn about our revenues and payroll, why we are different from our competitors, why profit is rising or falling. The dividends that we reap from the cleaning woman's attitude and from the other employees at every level, guarantee that there's a lot of opportunity for our business units to grow, profit, and endure over the years.

At Semco, we abolish manuals, procedures, and policies so that people are free to improvise, to soar, and to collect the moments of happiness that constitute genuine success. Because of our careful mix, because of the self-selection process that goes on, Semco has less than 1 percent turnover. We rarely fire anyone. In 2000 and 2001, a total of three people out of almost three thousand quit on their own.

To keep turnover low, we remind Semco employees to make sure that they are where they want to be, and to make sure that they are doing what they want to do. If they're not sure, we'll bend over backwards to find a completely different area or completely different type of work for them, just as we did for Lucia Kobayashi. Our motives are purely selfish. Unless we click with a worker, unless he latches onto something he is passionate about, our productivity won't be high. If someone is bored in his job, he should move on to something else, even if it means giving several options a try. Few organizations make an effort to find out whether a person has a calling. At Semco we try to encourage the process with several different programs.

One of them allows people to act like entrepreneurs within Semco. Called Lost in Space, it assumes that young recruits don't know what they want to do with their lives. The program is designed to help them decide by letting them roam through the company for a year. They do what they want to do, move when they want to move, go where their interests take them; work for one, three, or six different units. At the end of the year, anyone they've worked for can offer them a job, or they can seek an opening in an area that interests them.

If neither happens, we thank them for the year. We started this program because of my firm belief that under our current educational and economic system, a post adolescent or a twenty-two-year-old college graduate is in a poor position to make the life-altering decision of choosing a career. Young people are unduly influenced by what their parents expect of them, particularly when it comes to education and profession, and it's easy for them to choose a path that might not have been what they really wanted.

In our Lost in Space program, Rafael Tinoco, an eighteen-year-old computer hacker genius, was free to spend a year at the company doing as he wished while making himself interesting and useful to us. The difference between Semco and other companies is that we put young employees like Rafael in our non-territorial offices, where mutual contamination is guaranteed. When a teenager is seated next to our senior directors and surrounded by people of all backgrounds and ages, everyone will learn. When they all share a cappuccino, or overhear each other's conversations, they learn from each other. A training program or apprenticeship in a marketing or finance area only isolates a young person. We can't know where their real talent or real interest lies if they're restricted to one narrow area of specialization. If they only work in a designated spot, then senior people in the company might have limited contact with them or none at all. When everyone sits together in nonterritorial offices, they necessarily interact all the time.

Rafael's current interest lies in holography. That may lead to nothing, since we cannot currently see a connection to what we do. But hey—Rafael may change his interest, or find a niche for us in holography. The only thing I know is that we all learn very little if we have preconceived notions of training, careers, and business models that compel us to say, "This is the way we do things."

Rafael's story reminds me that I need to digress briefly to tell you about an ongoing project that has nothing and everything to do with the seven-day weekend. Having discovered that a lot of effort has to be put in by Semco into deprogramming adults, we at the Semco Foundation started an Institute for Advanced Learning called Lumiar (Portuguese for "to shed light on") and a school for children. It is based on the same tenets as Semco—freedom, self-determination and self-discipline, passion and love. This may sound woodstockish or summerhillian but its goal is the utmost of practicality and excellence: to effectively teach some of the accumulated knowledge of humankind to free-thinking children.

The teaching team is divided into two groups: Tutors and Masters. Tutors transmit tribal wisdom and hold hands. Then we have ninety-seven Masters for thirty kids who come from varied backgrounds—violinists, circus artists, mathematicians, dozens of university professors. Any one of them is an expert and has passion. The kids decide their disciplinary issues, and come to class if they want. It's counterproductive to attempt to educate a child who isn't interested in learning at that moment. And, like the company, we do 360-degree evaluations, including parents and the educators.

Our little ones tell us what they want to learn and eat; they decide on what penalties are appropriate (throwing books carried a "two days tied to a tree" sanction, which was lifted when the kids couldn't decide how to explain this to the guilty child's mother). So far, they are doing better in standardized tests than the norm. Lumiar has now taken over a public school and is expanding fast. Just as Semco is changing the way work works, Lumiar is changing the way the ABCs work.

End of digression. And the reason I'm so brazen about interrupting the flow here is that Semco wouldn't need weirdo programs like Lost in Space and the others if our educational system weren't so rotten.

Okay. Another program called Rush Hour MBA assembles every Monday at 6:00 P.M. It started as a productive way for people to use the time they would otherwise spend sitting in Sao Paulo's rush-hour traffic. Instead of wasting two hours commuting from one side of the city to the other, people can attend lectures and classes in our headquarters that last until rush hour is over. They still have to drive home, but the ride is much shorter and they have new ideas to think about on the way.

The program started on a very small scale but swiftly became very popular. Volunteers lead each session, suggest topics, bring up business trends, and share articles they've read or discuss current events. People with expertise expound on articles from the *Harvard Business Review, McKinsey Reports,* or last week's *Financial Times.* Now it includes people at Semco who are enrolled in training or graduate courses. They update their colleagues on what they've learned in more formal settings. We hoped that Rush Hour MBA would ignite change because it would prompt debate and new ideas. We think it also helps people develop their calling by exposing them to a wide variety of topics.

Other companies have similar executive education programs. General Electric operates a huge one with an enrollment nearly the size of a respectable graduate business school. It has professors on staff and a preset curriculum. Naturally, we want our program to be more rambling, free form, and loosely structured.

I have my own resolution to study two hours a day. I want to further my own education, but I mean to do it without rhyme or reason. In some respect, the goal of Rush Hour MBA is the same. I may study Jupiter today, and the Spanish Inquisition tomorrow. Anyone concerned with structure might think there's no discipline to that. I believe the two hours is my discipline. It won't count for anything because no school could grade my efforts, but after a year in which I may have studied a little biology, a little astronomy, a little history, I'll be better educated and better able to apply my knowledge to what I do every day.

This program also ensures I'll remain interested. If there were some control over how I studied, I'd probably give up rather than stay on a subject that bored me. That's the problem with control. It can cost the student his in-

MAKE IT INTERESTING AND THEY WILL COME.

terest, and to paraphrase the Hollywood film *Field of Dreams,* if you make it interesting, they will come.

We also have an internal hiring program called Family Silverware. The motivation here is to give preference to people we already know. It can create problems because talented employees are aware they can move to more challenging units. Their managers are often frustrated because, while they hope the worker will maximize his potential with them, other managers are constantly dangling better jobs in front of them. In hiring, we give internal candidates a discount over external candidates, usually a 30 percent rebate on the score necessary for the winning candidate. This differential makes up for the advantages our own people have: They know us, we know them, and we believe they can grow into the new job if they set their mind to it. That's worth 30 percent. It also makes it possible for people to change areas entirely, to try something that they might like better, and dip into their reservoirs of talent.

That's how Jose Violi became our CFO. He had none of the usual qualifications, yet he rose from within and surpassed people with wildly superior formal qualifications. Everyone quickly learned to respect the tiny, timid man who in minutes can cut through a complex business plan to get to its essence. Without Violi, we'd be in endless hot water, and yet, he'd have a hard time being hired at another company. He doesn't flaunt his power, doesn't market himself well, and is always ready to say he doesn't know something.

We can't train people to turn them into what we want. Mostly, we want nothing. We don't like training manuals, nor do we ask people where they want to be in five years. We want them to amble and ramble. If they happen to be on a fixed path, we'll gladly help them train for that, but instead of formal training, we encourage people to ask a colleague for explanations, demonstrations, and guidance. Information in any organization should be information on demand.

Henrique Oliveira, the food engineer in our machinery business unit, was hired after a collective interview with a panel of ten people drawn from across Semco. Most of them were people he'd eventually work with, and Henrique discovered that the process helped him decide whether he wanted to work with them, too. Hence, he wasn't surprised when he found himself leading a team that was accustomed to asking questions and questioning decisions.

On one occasion, a shop-floor worker thought it was strange that an important piece of equipment was being built without a filter and a waste pipe. The question prompted Henrique to reexamine the assembly plans. It took a few hours, but in the end it helped everyone on the team understand the reason they wouldn't be including important parts of the equipment at that time. The problem, Henrique realized, wasn't faulty specifications but rather that the instructions did not explain why a standard practice wasn't being followed.

This exercise wasn't an "exercise." It was part of an ongoing discovery process for both the organization and our workers. To go back to the scuba analogy that I used earlier: We want our people to strap on the air tanks, dive, enjoy the scenery, and then tell us about it. The company will learn something it wouldn't otherwise know. It would be worth discovering, for example, if we had left out a filter and waste pipe by mistake.

One good question and one good answer are services to all. A sure sign of a troubled company is one where employees don't care enough to ask and, if that's the case, they'll never care enough to fully deploy their talent. Just as curiosity is an antidote to boredom and indifference, the informed are more likely to remain interested, engaged, and alive with purpose. Even though it's not about money, that's a highly profitable outcome, no matter what day of the seven-day weekend it is.

- **Why hire the best and the brightest?**

- **Why are credentials so important?**

- **Why not hire the "wrong" candidate to see what happens?**

FIVE

WEDNESDAY

- Attend a board of directors' meeting.
- Dump a deal rather than pay a bribe.
- Tell the company it sucks.

MY BOARD RECENTLY TOLD me to get lost, take a hike, and otherwise make myself scarce. Let me set the scene for this not-so-unusual moment of brutal candor: I'd settled next to a junior marketing assistant on this particular day. Semco's board has nine seats, two of which are always open for the employees who sign up on a first-come, first-served basis.

The newcomers fell into the usual banter and joking that takes place at the beginning of these board meetings, and which belies the fury with which members later defend their points of view. For a first timer, these meetings are a heady and confusing mix of personal camaraderie and conceptual battles. One minute someone might be up in arms against our CFO, Jose Violi, about corporate expense allocations and in the next, fighting alongside him to reduce investments in a start-up. People and issues are almost never confused, so it is amusing to see individuals raising their voices at each other, and then pouring coffee for one another. The young marketer on my right probably felt like a spectator at a tennis match following each argument.

That's when I raised my concern over growth. We had just seen a graph showing that the company was set to grow yet another 42 percent after years of some 35 percent expansion per year. I told the others I was nostalgic for the sense of security and predictability that accompanied our cruising altitude years, and that I felt perturbed at the idea that we now have thousands of employees.

Certainly it feeds my ego to employ that many people at Semco. It also vindicates my conviction that our model of democracy and freedom in the workplace will lend itself to bigger companies. But growth per se is scary. We don't fear losing control, because we've come to grips with that. Yet I worry that our culture is diluting too quickly, that we have two or three new employees for every veteran.

The board members reassured me to a degree. They believe that our growth is not internally induced and that we aren't pushing the company past its organic size. The growth we're experiencing results from growing markets or market share, both of which should be sustainable. They made the usual comments about growth being necessary for clout, scale of economy, geographical and human resource distribution, career perspectives, and competitor comparisons. The goal is to make Semco a $1 billion company in five years.

Their final argument was the most persuasive of them all: To act on my reservations, Semco would have to artificially cap the growth of its business units. It would mean exerting control, thus undermining the democracy and freedom we so flamboyantly advocate, all because Ricardo was getting goose bumps over our growth rate.

Well, I concede that the majority shareholder obstructing his company's growth is not standard fare for board meetings, but I still felt myself turning red at the smiles and teasing.

If you want slow growth, head for your mountain ranch and watch the grass grow during your long hikes, one of the board members said half-jokingly. I got his point. The botanical garden that I'm having put in at the ranch is scheduled to be ready in 2017. Therefore, at least from a horticultural perspective, my concerns about rapid growth are assuaged by a stand of Sequoias, which since they are among the slowest growing, longest lived, and most massive trees on earth, should mature in time for my great grandchild's wedding.

After putting me in my place, the board turned to other issues, leaving critical questions unanswered: What is success, and what does it have to do with money or growth? Why are we so obsessed about it? Why is success a natural culmination of talent and calling if it is measured in numbers?

GROWTH THAT KILLS

The word "success" begs for a definition so we can understand what we strive for. It's a deceptively easy word to toss around but a difficult one to comprehend. In a business context, most people define success as growth, profit, product acceptance, and quality. But if we apply this to personal life, those definitions do not hold up.

If growth is necessary to success, we need a means to guarantee that it continues. Still, nothing grows indefinitely. In nature, growth is only temporary. The tallest trees are the first to get struck by lightning. When I asked once at a medical conference if anyone knew of an organism that enjoyed perpetual growth, someone said cancer and pointed out that it eventually kills its host.

I'm not ready to concede that business has invented the only organism—the company—that grows endlessly and benignly. Nor would I say there is always value in endless growth. Is an evergreen tree superior to a tree ablaze with bright yellow leaves in the fall? Is McDonald's better than the Five Flies Restaurant in Amsterdam, which has remained the same size and has been owned by the same family for hundreds of years?

I once took a physics course, at the end of which the professor had only one question: How far can you go into a forest? The correct answer was midway. Go beyond that and you're leaving the forest. I think of this when I consider my company's growth. Are we growing or merely leaving the forest? There's no such thing as perpetual growth. Yet that's what many traditional business people crave.

But what is growth meant to achieve? If Oxford University is so successful, then why isn't there a branch in Washington, D.C.? If a symphony is successful with 120 musicians, why isn't it better with 600?

The minute I hear conventional explanations for business practices, like the idea that companies are required to grow, that profit is paramount, I know I'm encountering calcified thinking. I immediately want to ask why. Why greater wealth? So that we can make even more money, and then be obliged to earn more beyond that? Why is growth necessary beyond the minimum natural expansion of the market being served?

Why do we have to make more money every quarter or face being downgraded by analysts on Wall Street? Because Wall Street needs to guarantee income to pension funds, which in turn finance ever-increasing numbers of retired people? Because it must compensate for too many bad bets on start-ups, dot-coms and mature players that are no longer ready for prime time? Because it has hired too many MBAs who make too much money and drive costs ever higher?

None of these is a convincing reason for relentless growth.

And why does growth create a competitive advantage? Calcified thinking would point to strategic positioning, mass, and global deployment. Why isn't remaining about the same in size and perfecting what we do more advantageous than hiring new people that we do not know, opening new plants that will have a long learning curve, and losing sight of what we've already learned to do best?

Every year, there are dozens of telecommunications companies like Global Crossing, accounting firms like Arthur Andersen, retailers like Kmart, or car companies like Volvo and Rover that overextend themselves, lose control over their businesses, and end up broke or sold to competitors.

Profit beyond the minimum is not essential for survival. In any event, an organization doesn't really need profit beyond what is vital for working capital and the small growth that is essential for keeping up with the customers and competition. Excess profit only creates another imbalance. To be sure, it enables the owner or CEO to commission a yacht. But then employees will wonder why they should work so the owner can buy a boat.

And plowing profits back into the company is akin to saying the jail has too many empty cells so it's time to round up more prisoners. Or that since there are extra violins, let's find more violinists for the orchestra. Ultimately, balance suffers.

Upsetting the seesaw causes problems of its own. A deficit can be deadly, but a surplus can wreak havoc, too. Someone will start spending that surplus, and it may lead a company to build more factories than it can sustain, lease new headquarters that aren't necessary, or acquire a company that doesn't fit.

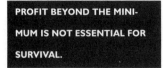

PROFIT BEYOND THE MINIMUM IS NOT ESSENTIAL FOR SURVIVAL.

An organization can remain small and focused for centuries. Witness Bologna University, the Vienna Philharmonic, Orthodox churches, Dutch schools, or Scandinavian paper companies, all of which are many hundreds of years old.

SHIPPING WATER

Another argument follows the analogy that all boats float on a rising tide and, therefore, everyone will do better when company profits increase. Right? Wrong. With a few exceptions among senior management, it is absolutely untrue that employees make more over the years as the company grows. One of the rarely examined policies of large operations is the expedience of exploiting turnover to substitute expensive employees with cheaper labor. In the case of global companies, this can be brutally simple: A plant in Texas is moved to cheaper Ireland, then moved again to India, and lastly, to Vietnam. Employees in this growing company are far worse off, it seems to me, now that the average hourly rate has dropped from $22 in the United States to 21 cents in Southeast Asia. Or maybe I'm missing something!

At Semco, we've concentrated instead on finding the right organic size for each of our markets. Growth and profit are rarely an issue. We concentrate on the process and look only for growth that can endure.

Not long ago, we ran into a situation that brought the issue of growth versus values to the surface. We'd entered a joint effort with a giant multinational company to sell an HR consulting package to a leading national oil company. The multinational did the selling, and we came along as a preferred partner. After almost a dozen presentations, our consortium was awarded the $30 million contract. About $6 million was ours.

Much to our dismay, when our representatives went to settle details with the multinational, we were informed that the sale had involved a kickback to one of the client's directors. Our people were astounded. Not only did they not know about the arrangement but they were shocked that this prestigious and well-branded entity had consented. Most notably, they were upset that this firm didn't know (or care) that Semco was famous throughout Brazil for its vocal anticorruption position, and thus was the wrong party for such business practices. Indeed, we had previously provided evidence that led to prosecutions and convictions for extortion and bribery on several occasions. We weren't about to participate in a kickback scheme.

The multinational's directors were adamant about the deal, and encouraged our people to accept the circumstances. These were just the facts of life, they said. One of their executives, who knew its potential impact on our company, asked pointedly: "Is this the reply that Semco will give in the future to all such situations?" He knew that our market would be severely limited if we were to follow the straight and narrow path. Huge business opportunities were emerging in the very large, and very corrupt, oil industry.

Danilo Saicali, Semco's CEO, and Jose Violi, our CFO, answered simultaneously, their e-mails crossing. Danilo said that there is no issue of past, present, or future, that this was Semco's policy. End of story. Violi, although well aware of the impact, was equally emphatic: "Return the order."

The multinational in question has a credo and mission statement that are beautiful to behold. By contrast, we write nothing down. While this might sound corny or self-aggrandizing, we think that the journey through life—either personal or corporate—provides snapshots and memories that, upon reflection, tell us how happy we were and how true to ourselves we have been. We have a common denominator with those accompanying us on the trip, and we need to feel good about the road we have traveled.

Even though we could be much bigger, we're convinced that rejecting such opportunities strengthens our management practices and earns us respect. That makes it easier to attract the talent that we need at all levels and then, finally, to generate better business, including increased size and profit.

So it is not about being virgins in a brothel. Rather, insistence on high ethical standards is simply good for business.

For those who want growth at any price, there are mergers and acquisitions; just another form of keeping score on the big board. Legions of lawyers, consultants, and auditors have made fortunes from mergers and acquisitions. No words ring as musically in their ears as "due diligence," the process of digging into the depths of a company's psyche and ancient filing cabinets, searching

AN INSISTENCE ON HIGH ETHICAL STANDARDS IS SIMPLY GOOD FOR BUSINESS.

for lies, risk, and other grist for the negotiators' mill. Where does all this frenzy for combining two into one, for takeovers and buyouts originate? What does it say about growth?

Why would two companies decide they'd be better off as one? The calcified, conventional answer is that it increases clout and competitiveness, while reducing duplication. Theoretically, then, it would be even better for three, four, or five companies to join forces.

Under this assumption, the ideal industry would have two or three companies or groups of companies in each business niche. No more. They'd achieve the maximum possible scale economies, leverage, and technological capacity. But you'll notice that these dreamed-of gains, so convincingly extolled at merger announcements by two beaming CEOs, rarely if ever materialize. Then there's the opinion of those who can attest that it's hell to work in a recently merged company. And why must these new entities merge further, until the Big Eight become Four, or the Seven Sisters become Three? We seem to be saying that happiness on the board will occur only when the Seven Sisters have turned into twins.

Please.

Mergers are about growth and profit (or in the case of WorldCom, funding future acquisitions). But many times they are also a remedy of last resort for bad management. Companies with mistakes to cover up are the first ones in search of a merger. Companies that are doing beautifully are usually only interested in acquisitions.

Corporations go through cycles of growth and retrenching, what I call corporate yo-yo dieting. Companies that expand continually are companies that grow fat. Then they're forced to diet, or downsize in "corp" speak, until they can grow again and reengineer (a new body in ninety days!), merge and acquire other companies (weightlifting and muscle training) until the cycle starts anew, and they're forced to reduce again (lose twenty pounds in six weeks!). No wonder people who work in these places are perplexed, weary, and soft.

We know that's unhealthy, especially when companies expand but do not grow taller, or find new markets. Yet so many business leaders believe that no growth is equally disastrous.

In the last eight years, none of our businesses grew less than 22 percent per year. One grew an average of 44 percent every year. But rather than rejoicing in healthy expansion, so much growth alarms me.

At Semco RGIS, for example, we face a dilemma. Growing quickly is strategic, because we have rapidly become the market leaders in that business. National stature, which means launching in five to seven new cities every year, is critical to servicing large global retailers like Wal-Mart or JC Penney. On the other hand, hiring in a hurry, shoring up the back office, finding experienced front line supervisors, and setting aside the huge amounts of capital that growth consumes is a challenging proposition.

RGIS, under Marcio Batoni, has experienced phenomenal growth of 50 to 80 percent every year. The rest of us are constantly trying to hold Marcio back because we think a slower rate of growth will ensure quality, not to mention our sanity. But Marcio is convinced that a Semco presence in every major South American city is the only guarantee against encroaching competition. We'll see . . .

THE FORTUNATE 500

If growth is not the barometer of success, then we need a new way to determine when a company is doing well or badly. One sensible approach is to ask stockholders, employees, clients, suppliers, and community for their opinions, producing a three-dimensional picture of strengths and weaknesses. We have such a scorecard at Semco, one that will enable us to compare progress, anticipate trouble, and tweak our priorities.

After all, the goal is to exchange revenue-based evaluations for something much more complex and revealing. By evaluating success from everyone's unique point of view, we believe we'll land on the new list of companies that unite sustainability with all-around gratification. Let's call this list the Fortunate 500.

Over the years, we've all been dismayed to see companies that appeared to be healthy falter and even implode—IBM in the 1990s, Ford in 2002, Apple or Netscape in their early days, Enron, Arthur Andersen, and WorldCom more recently. Clearly, a balance sheet, a stock market price, and customer satisfaction ratings aren't enough to indicate how a company is really doing.

Likewise, if public businesses are so difficult to assess, the same can be said of nongovernmental organizations (NGOs), libraries, and hospitals. We need a new way of evaluating companies, a 360-degree, comprehensive measuring gauge of how well an organization is doing.

The numbers are a useful place to start. It's vital to know what companies sell, spend on marketing, or earn as profit. Dig down and determine their debt levels and ratings, as well. All of these are an important part of the "Barometer." But the debacle of fallen companies that had earlier been regarded as successes demonstrates that numbers aren't everything. Most executives agree that responses from customers are important. Even so, there's a catch. They just don't know how to ask the right questions, or get the client interested in answering them.

It's not surprising that automakers and airlines have changed so little in the last fifty years and find it so awfully hard to make money consistently. None of the big U.S. car companies or airlines has ever enjoyed other than intermittent consecutive profits. Just look at the questions they ask their end users: Is this year's model better than last year's? Is the car dealer's service satisfactory? Was an airfare better than that of competitors? Does the company fly through the right hubs?

These are the same status quo questions that the U.S. Postal Service asked its constituency in the 1980s, before UPS and FedEx came along. Or GTE asked its telephone users before Nokia appeared. Or Philips asked its portable radio users before the Walkman walked in.

Incorrect questions will generate incorrect answers, followed by misguided directions and a mistaken assumption of how well an organization is doing.

Questions bordering on the absurd are more useful.

- **What would you like your car to run on? Answer: Solar energy, electricity, gas, helium, but not fossil fuels.**

- **How would you like to change a flat tire? In no more than four minutes, without dirtying my hands and running risks in unsafe neighborhoods.**

- **What food would you like on an airplane? Something that I can select from a preset menu and is cooked to order.**

- **When would you like a big parcel delivered? Next day, guaranteed.**

- **How would you like to use a phone? Absurd answer to an absurd question: While I jog, without having to dial, carry equipment, or use batteries.**

- **How would you like your cassette tape player to work? Ridiculous answer at the time: While I walk in the park, or by downloading music while walking in the park, without cables or batteries, just by saying what I want (absurd now).**

Asking the right questions, even if you are not prepared for the answers, is fundamental to our Barometer.

Marcio Batoni has created a useful customer survey that is open ended and conducted immediately following completion of an inventory when interest and action are simultaneous. It asks users to stipulate their ideal service, how quickly they need inventory results, and how few of our people they would like to see in their stores. We've had requests that would have been absurd just a few years ago, including downloading data every two minutes, which we do, or taking inventory in a supermarket full of shopping customers, which we also do.

Another piece of this puzzle is employees.

If we have a moral code, it's our insistence on trust. We want Semco employees to have faith in their company. We measure that with a survey asking our employees to tell us anonymously once a year what they think of the company, its management, its future. We circulate questionnaires and ask them whether they feel like coming to work on Monday morning, whether they trust their leaders, and whether they believe everything we say in our internal and external communications. Since 1996, between 85 and 94 percent of replies have been in the top brackets—good and great. And those percentages have increased almost every year, indicating that leaders take the responses seriously.

The ratings that result from these questionnaires give us an invaluable picture of year-to-year performance. How many companies want to hear those answers, much less publish them? Yet that's just what we'll do at Semco. In hopes of convincing people and markets that transparency pays, we are planning to begin publishing survey findings (our Barometer) together with our financial reports. It will provide a new level of accountability and increase trust from minority shareholders, customers, employees, and suppliers.

Rarely queried suppliers, consultants, and independent contractors need to be brought in from the cold, too. So once a year we invite dozens of them to tour Semco, and ask them pointed questions about our performance. Since most can't be expected to talk candidly, we provide them with anonymous questionnaires, which can be tallied instantly for immediate discussion. The result of these evaluations will also be published in our Barometer.

Organizations must be accountable to the public, and they should comply with realistic regulations. So scrutiny should also focus on the world beyond business—environmentalists, legal protection agencies, government, and all sorts of NGOs. Today, NGOs can protest outside G-8 Summits (and see their supporters or opponents get dragged off to jail), and present reports to the public. It is a bit more difficult to affect the corporate world. Certainly, companies pay increasing lip service to social responsibility to an extent that has become a cliché. Social balance sheets are becoming so common that they all look alike: They describe environmental compliance, parks and rivers a company has cleaned up, schools for the poor that a corporation has financed, and the thousands of hours of training in social responsibility furnished to their employees. Soon, you won't be able to tell one social balance sheet from another, just as has happened to credos and mission statements.

By adding this dimension to the Barometer, we are adding a vital link to accountability. Sustainable practices in companies are closely related to the laws and social issues that NGOs, government agencies, and the general public are concerned with. If no company is an island, dealing at close quarters with groups who see companies in the light of the greater good is vital to success.

We're creating our Barometer as a definition of success. By combining numbers and people, customers and suppliers, and government agencies and NGOs, we hope to produce a well-rounded evaluation of the word "success." If we can find sustainability and gratification for all these groups, we'll have an all-encompassing success. And that'll make Semco one of the Fortunate 500.

And what barometer do we use to determine success or happiness for individuals, even the richest of them? I once spoke to a billionaire's group at the Ritz Hotel in Paris. I faced the one hundred highest net worth customers of the (then) Chase Manhattan Bank. These men, royalty of the coin, came together to ponder, meditate on their condition and, as two of them confessed, to monitor their wives' shopping (I'm not responsible for the sexist division of activities!). What interested me, as I surveyed them from the podium, was the motivation that took them to the office on Monday morning. I asked them to tell me why they were in business. The reply, laconic and unadorned, lacked poetry but made up with power: to make money. The more politically correct among them embellished this as "enhancing shareholder wealth."

I followed up by asking the group what their goal had been when they started out. Mostly self-made men, they had set numerical targets such as $10 million, $100 million, and even $1 billion. It's interesting; why is it that no one sets targets of $83 million? And what if they set $100 million as a goal but fall short and achieve only $83 million? Do they become disillusioned, angry, frustrated? What is it about these resonant, round, cabalistic numbers that speaks to people's self-esteem? The intriguing part, moreover, is that no matter what the local currency was wherever I've pursued my unscientific investigation, whether it was strong or weak, hyper-inflated or rock solid, whether it was called dinars, pound sterling, or yen; one of these big, occult numbers was always attached. There was no connection to intrinsic value. The sound of the number overrode the economic sense of the currency.

That proved to me that these were tribal, ego-related sums, not business necessities. To a tee, these men had all grandly exceeded their goals. So what took them to the office after that, once their targets had been achieved? Something did.

I found the same to hold true at a program I had earlier attended at Harvard. Fully one-third of my class had made their riches and then sold out. Of these, no less than 88 percent had eventually purchased another business. Money was not the object. In essence, these people were in business to dip into their reservoirs of talent, that pool of inherent interests and skills that is unique to us all. They dip to make themselves feel alive, to provide purpose and identity, to satisfy their egos with the trappings of status, to feel that their lives were worth living. Never for the money.

That's why any discussion of happiness brings us to wealth. Somehow we tend to merge these two even when we realize it's a mistake.

I have a theory about wealth. For it to be relevant, I need you to imagine that you are a multimillionaire, and perhaps a few readers qualify for real. Either way, I believe that the maximum personal wealth is $12 million, not a penny more. How's that for a cabalistic number? The twelve apostles of Christ and the twelve months of the year. I've actually done some calculations with economists to justify this deliberately provocative number. It hinges on the fact that all millionaires are the same.

Blame it on Leonardo da Vinci. He worried about proportions between man, space, and the divine. The rules that Leonardo identified as he drew, painted, and invented are the ones that hold people to $12 million. I call it the Da Vinci Constraint.

Da Vinci's friend Paccioli made the point in 1509 with his book *Da Divina Proportione*. Da Vinci illustrated this book with many drawings, one of which nearly everyone knows—the one with the bearded man with two pairs of arms outstretched, squaring the circle. What I call the Da Vinci Constraint, therefore, is a way of applying that theory to wealth. It has to respect proportion to be useful.

Humanity is limited in how much it can indulge, how many meals a person can eat, how many toys a child can play with, how much horsepower a car can generate before it becomes airborne. A neighbor of mine in Sao Paulo built a house that reminds me of a South American dictator's compound. He may have spent his entire allotment of $12 million on the house. But now his problem is Leonardo, who points out that a human cannot possibly feel at ease in such a disproportionate house. Certainly my neighbor can live there, open it to photographers from design magazines, and be admired from afar. But in winter he'll huddle in the tiny TV room on the second floor, withdrawing from the cavernous rooms to seek a more human scale.

That's what the $12 million does. It gives you the access to a large city house or apartment, a beach house, a mountain cottage, three cars, and even a helicopter, if you must. Three meals a day, a personal trainer to do away with their side effects, clubs, spas, elegant European travel. Seven or eight servants, dandy schools for the kids, opera tickets galore, and accounts at Donna Karan. And that's why all millionaires are the same after that sum. More money buys nothing that they really need. That doesn't mean they stop. Accumulating money is a way to keep score, but ultimately the Da Vinci Constraint prevails; and the rich keep getting richer for the same reason all people get up and go to work—they seek to make use of their talent.

Collecting money is a talent, but not necessarily a higher talent, and is like amassing any other item—stamps, Tiffany lamps, or bottle caps. By definition, no collector can ever be happy. There will always be a piece, a unit, a set that can't be had.

On a trip to Bangkok, I met a man who had made his fortune in tomatoes, import and export, and steel. He was proud that the flight over his tomato fields took forty minutes.

We went to dinner. A chain-smoker, my host was said to light one match a day when he got out of bed. With every cigarette he would light the next. Throughout dinner he did not once put out a cigarette, eating with one hand and smoking with the other. As we left the restaurant, his driver appeared out of nowhere in a World War II–era Mercedes stretch limo. What a relic, I exclaimed, as he explained offhand that he owned a "vertical collection" of Mercedes. I knew from wine collecting that vertical meant an example from every production year.

As we parted, he mentioned that he liked to fly the same airline I was taking to London. But how did he manage a fourteen-hour flight without smoking, I asked.

"Oh, I buy first class," he explained. But so did I, and I still couldn't smoke, I replied.

"No, sir," he smiled wanly between puffs. "You fly first class. I buy first class." He regularly booked all sixteen seats in First Class so that he could close the section and smoke to his heart's content (and by choosing an Asian-owned airline, many of which still permit smoking). So much for $12 million and Da Vinci. The man's sense of proportion was grotesquely distorted.

Not many people are as far gone, but organizations are prone to a similar mania. That is why we so often stand in awe in atrium headquarters, gaping at the cathedral ceilings and all the attributes that pass for solidity, prestige, and making a statement. It's all a show that has nothing to with operating a sustainable business organization.

THE TOMATO TYCOON AND the men at the Ritz sat at the pinnacle of pioneering psychologist Abraham Maslow's tower, the one built from the theory that motivation climbs a ladder of needs from the basic—like food and sex—to the highest, which he regarded as involving self-actualization by way of realizing one's human potential. At the conference, I asked them what they did with the extra money that had rolled in through the cashier's window. They spoke of the need to return it to society, to preserve peace and promote justice, to help cure disease, to make the landscape greener, and to put more books on library shelves. Surely, I'd say, if these were their needs, it was something that they did in silence, for inner relief. How many of them had once dedicated a hospital or museum wing named The Anonymous Wing? Not surprisingly the reply was none. Then perhaps their grants are nothing but ego trips. Would they have donated if their name weren't on the opera seat, the brochure, or the zoo gate? Self-aggrandizement and the lure of social status are hard to resist.

But the easy replies about money are specious. It all has very little to do with cash. A list highlighting the Happiest would have no names in common with one listing the Wealthiest (even if *People* magazine were doing the work behind it).

The same is true for companies. Cash on hand, revenue,

and profits are wonderful indeed, but say precious little if taken on their own. If Enron had stayed in the black would that have made it any less sleazy? Of course not. Profits must be judged as moral or immoral by how they are earned and how they are disposed. Without a new barometer, we are left with the old barometer—profit for its own sake, regardless of whether it is sustainable or ultimately ruinous. But over the course of a seven-day weekend when a reservoir of talent is tapped, a calling is found, a true, well-rounded definition of success is established, people may realize they're working not for the money but literally working *for* and *on* themselves. And what a liberating realization that is. Organizations and people need other ways to measure how well they're doing. It might create a sense of energizing relief for individuals, and push companies toward the realm where sustainability and personal gratification meet profitability. That would earn them a slot on the Fortunate 500.

- Why grow at all?

- Why not shrink?

- Why is money so important?

SIX

THURSDAY

- Make a fool of yourself in front of the customer.
- Share confidential information.
- Do nothing.

SINCE THURSDAY DERIVES FROM Thor's day, the Viking God of thunder, put on your body armor, mount up, move out and . . .

Imagine an army general convincing his superiors that he has a glut of provisions and thus needs to enlist more soldiers. Profit is highly important to us at Semco, and we're as avid about it as a general is about his supplies. If provisions run out, his soldiers will die. If a company ceases to make money, it too will die. But armies are not created to feed soldiers, just as companies don't generate income just so they can hire more employees. Food fuels the soldiers and keeps them going. Yet to serve as more than mere gun fodder, they must have a higher purpose, a reason for going through boot camp and charging the enemy in battle. Like workers or millionaires, they must answer to a higher calling. This is where profit and purpose meet and, unfortunately for most organizations, it's a head-on Humvee wreck.

For companies, a calling is the mission, and it is partnered with its brother-in-arms, credo. Together, they seek to explain why a company exists, where it is going, and what principles it holds dear. They are beautiful documents—and largely useless, because the high-flown words can simply be replaced with everyday deeds that embody what the company stands for.

Genuine, organic values must come from the ground up. Relinquishing control nurtures these values, because they'll then flourish in organizations like moss on rocks. They become integral to a company to such an extent that no one can tell who decided what or determined which way the company would do things.

The mission and credo terminology is borrowed from the military, and the deficiencies in the military analogy illustrate why grassroots, deed-driven values are preferable and successful. It's absurd to argue that troops won't obey orders that they don't understand or agree with. History shows us that warriors have bravely fought and died for no other reason than that their leaders commanded them to make the ultimate sacrifice. Consequently, for the military, mission and credo are primarily public relations gimmicks, although they have some limited utility as personnel management tools. Convincing a twenty-year-old soldier that she should give her life for God and country is an easier sell than presenting it as the price for General Shinbone's third star or for a politician's reelection.

Dressed up in red, white, and blue; shod in desert boots; and draped in camouflage cloth; mission and credos are appealing to the general public. As a result, companies love them and readily adopt the military model and mind-set when dealing with their "troops," including customers, suppliers, investors, government regulators, and employees. The whiff of gunpowder glamorizes an otherwise humdrum process, conceals the command-and-control tactics, and silences critics. In due course, companies convince themselves that their mission and credos are unique, fundamental, and awe inspiring.

In short, they start believing their own propaganda. I once conducted a workshop for fifty-six CEOs of *Fortune* 500 companies. I asked the participants to use a pencil to write in capital letters their company beliefs statement, the values that went into it, the credo that resulted. When they went out for a coffee break, I shuffled the cards on which they'd written their answers. Then I laid out the cards at random on their tables. When they returned, most of the participants agreed that if not for small features of the handwriting, they couldn't differentiate among the credo statements.

Few can avoid pious platitudes when formulating a mission statement. You know what I mean, things like, "We provide the best service from the happiest employees at the most competitive price to satisfied customers, while enchanting shareholders." It's as if every time I meet someone new, I said, "Hi, I'm Ricardo Semler. I strive to be all that I can be, and I want you to be utterly happy to meet me."

What is left, then, if mission and credo are bullshit? Quite a lot, starting with what we stand for, the way we do things, the facts on the ground, the way we are perceived, and the satisfaction and success of those involved. In other words, judge us by what we do, rather than what we say we do. Judge us by standards drawn from a peaceful, civilized, cooperative, and humane society of equals, not those of a highly efficient killing machine that is designed to slay enemies, wreck property, and capture territory.

MOVING AN ORGANIZATION OR business ahead by virtue of what its people stand for and the deeds they do means removing obstacles like official policies, procedural constraints, and relentless milestones, all of which are established to pursue quarterly or otherwise temporary success on a business battlefield. It means giving up control, and allowing employees to manage themselves. It means trusting workers implicitly, sharing power and information, encouraging dissent, and celebrating true democracy.

Few things are harder for managers, executives, shareholders, and owners to embrace. While less bloodthirsty than the military battle cries that inspire them, corporate mission statements and credos are nothing more than feeble attempts to force workers to look in one direction. They dictate to employees why they should get up in the morning and go to work. "Here's your purpose, and it had better fit perfectly with the company's goals." In its most cynical form, it's like telling soldiers they must follow orders blindly. The idea is to pound any independent thought out of their heads at boot camp and pack them onto aircraft carriers or B-52s, otherwise they'll start to wonder whether they're really doing the right thing.

Yet within a company, truly sustainable profit, growth, and quality will happen only when employees feel it's worthwhile to get up for work. That won't happen if their outlook on the world is already shaped and restricted by a company's mission statement. They have much more time to think about what they're doing than a soldier in the heat of battle does.

I once met the grandson of a man who had manufactured trolley cars in Boston. The grandfather knew what his mission was—producing the best trolley cars on the planet. So enamored was he of his product that he determined that every cent of profit would be reinvested by a trust fund into trolley cars. His descendants thus lost everything, because their attorneys could not break his ironclad will. While he was alive, he was the prescient general. After he was gone, he became a maligned Napoleon Bonaparte.

A few years ago, it was popular for business gurus to equate companies with armies, and so a barrage of military paradigms such as marketing blitz, flanking attack, Sun Tzu's war strategies, the business wit and wisdom of Von Clausewitz, and endless bomb, bullet, and ballistic similes became the rage.

Today, as geopolitics becomes hotter, those same gurus have cooled down and equate a well-run company to a symphony orchestra. I must say, I prefer the change. An orchestra brings together individuals with initiative, discipline, and love of their art. These musicians join forces to create something beautiful that cannot occur without cooperation and participation.

Yet there are countless hours of self-discipline, difficult passages that must be mastered, autocratic maestros to deal with, and the usual amount of bickering, backstabbing, and quibbling over compensation.

The other advantage of the orchestra analogy is the comparison of a single individual directing 120 musicians with the 5 to 15, manager-to-employee ratio within most business organizations. Why the difference? Because in a symphony, professional musicians are playing a common score. Within a company, that score would be the mission statement.

But wait a minute. Isn't the mission the goal? And isn't an orchestra's goal to make music for an audience while also seeking personal growth and gratification as musicians? Can you keep a first-rate violinist in an orchestra that plays the same piece over and over like a cruise ship band?

A company's reason for existing is no different than that of an orchestra. For one, it's the product or service. For the other, it's the musical expression of emotion and ideas. Believe it or not, manufacturing a bus is similar to playing Mozart in the park. Both have a purpose, a system, and people who take the product to a waiting public.

But the mission varies. At times the mission of an orchestra is to take classical music to the widest audience possible. Witness the Three Tenors—three pudgy gentlemen performing cantina songs in kitsch concerts backed by bloated orchestras. Is this a good way to serve a mission? If the mission is to bring opera to the masses, absolutely.

At other times, the mission of the orchestra may be to stretch its limits, to indulge in a conductor's fantasy, to introduce new composers or works, or to showcase its members' virtuosity. So it should be with companies. Organizations must help workers indulge their interests and talents by seeking the same professional growth and satisfaction as musicians.

Most people would be wary about working for a company that doesn't define itself, has no mission statement, no plan. But at Semco, we have neither a mission statement, nor a credo. We do have a survival manual, and it tells employees to customize Semco to their wishes. If asked why Semco exists, those of us at the company will rely on the same answer we'd give about ourselves: We're not entirely sure, but it has to do with collective gratification and a reason to live and work.

PEER CONTROL

With nothing but intuitive values in place, trust becomes a fundamental part of our process. Some business practices make this difficult, however. Telling people they are trusted and then auditing them breeds insecurity. They know they're under some suspicion, that they've been subjected to a sort of Napoleonic code declaring everyone guilty until proven innocent.

At Semco, we don't require expense accounts because of what they say about character. They're insulting for two reasons. They imply that a worker did not really take a taxi for the company, and if she did, that we question her judgment about it.

We've learned that peer control is as effective as reporting and auditing. If people know there is no auditing or official policing, they're more aware of their own behavior and activity around them. They'll know that trust is in jeopardy if accounting is fraudulent or sloppy; they'll watch for theft because they know there is no security department filling that role.

We massage our truth index all the time, creating an environment where documents, memos, and reports to customers or clients are honest and representative. Many times I've watched as people reviewing draft reports and memos send them back with a note saying "Don't forget to add this or that," in an effort to better cultivate truth.

We once had an employee who was in the habit of telling customers he couldn't make a meeting because he was calling from the United States. He'd say this on the phone in front of colleagues, as if he thought this was normal and acceptable. But it bothered many people, and many of them mentioned it to me. This kind of mistrust is

EXPENSE ACCOUNTS ENCOURAGE DISTRUST AND CHEATING. ABOLISH THEM.

the bacteria that creates office politics. Semco has a low level of rumor, gossip, and politicking because our system doesn't lend itself to it, and the germs of mistrust don't proliferate as they would elsewhere.

Yet offering complete trust can also backfire. It's a chance you have to take when military control is chucked out the window.

When Semco launched RGIS, we brought in managers from the United States and Mexico. One was a real dynamo, a man with two decades of experience in the inventory business. He was doing a bang-up job when suddenly an unusual American Express bill arrived at our offices. Apparently this manager had been powerless to stop his wife from regularly overdrawing his company credit card. He'd left her back home in his native country and had taken up with a Brazilian woman. His angry wife took her revenge with the American Express card, until the manager faced a debt worth nearly two years' salary. It all happened very fast, but another company with stricter controls would probably have discovered the problem sooner. Skeptics could argue that this is a definite drawback to our open system. But we still haven't added oversight.

In the case of the manager, we faced a difficult decision. We needed his talents, and he'd been a stalwart executive. But he had also known that his wife was using his corporate card and hadn't told anyone. He'd hoped to cover the debt by selling property at home, but it didn't happen. Someone suggested turning the debt into a long-term loan, others worried about such a precedent. Our honor system had to be preserved, so we fired the manager, paid his moving expenses home, and wrote off the debt. We felt it was the best we could do.

A LOSE-LOSE

It's rare for a company to reject internal audits. But audits are designed to seek out breaches of trust. Almost all big companies have external auditors who inspect the books and review procedures to guarantee to shareholders that an independent entity has verified business claims. But the main activity is an inspection designed to ensure that everyone is following the rules.

Auditing is also used to ensure uniformity; inspecting is a tool for control. It's a lose-lose situation: If you are inspecting to ensure uniformity, then you are using it for control. If it is because you believe people will do wrong, then it is mistrust.

At Semco, any company that is 100 percent owned by us is not audited at all, internally or externally. Further, about half of our joint venture partners, all of which have strict auditing rules at their headquarters, have accepted our philosophy and don't audit our units, either.

No single person or group at Semco sets our common denominator or philosophies. No one (least of all me) has ever said, "Our common denominators will be honesty, trust, integrity."

So where does the essence of Semco originate?

From an organization that exposes workers to all of its different aspects and guarantees them a degree of mobility among the parts, so they will find a niche and not feel the need to look for a better life elsewhere.

We have your new life here, somewhere; it's in the job you were hired for, or the project you stumbled across, or in another unit in another building.

The day may arrive when that employee has spent fifteen or twenty years with Semco, and he's lived through seven different corporate lives, and has become an enormous asset. He's seen us do things seven different ways, and helped us succeed five times and fail twice.

Now I ask him to sit next to a twenty-one-year-old recent hire because he has something to teach him. They both learn, and so do I. And I'm left with people and lessons that aren't part of the world of mergers, reengineering, and turnover at other businesses—a shared culture and a shared set of minimum common denominators. "Minimum" is a critical part of the phrase, since even the smallest common denominator says that we're all here for the same reason.

Employees may have their own agenda and their own careers to consider, but the common denominator anchors all of us to the company. So now, whatever the company may do, I have the seeds of sustainability. I have something that will endure through turnover, cannibalizing, and time. And it's not a set of mission statements, credos, or values that I have decreed from a mountaintop. It's the philosophy that working together for years has instilled in people.

This naturally evolving and shared culture bonds people within a company, and it's founded on trust. You cannot have integrity, dissent, respect, or open communication without it. You must believe those features are constructive, even when they are sometimes painful. That only works if people trust each other, and trust the company. (Simply working the word "trust" into the mission statement won't cut it.)

A company that lacks integrity will eventually lose its best employees. Some will quit, others will stay and be "dumbed down." Anyone who stays will disengage emotionally, and soon will be a candidate for motivational seminars. But a company can't expect integrity from its employees until they see it in the organization. People need to have faith and pride in what a company promises to its customers, includes in contracts, or touts in its advertising. If they know there are falsehoods or deceptions, their willingness to associate with the company diminishes. Soon they'll be working there just for the paycheck, and be embarrassed to tell anyone.

I'm often asked: How do you control a system like this?

Answer: I don't. I let the system work for itself.

I am sure that if somebody in the company decides that the only way to compete in a business is by paying a 10 percent kickback, the Semco system will choke on the idea before it emerges. That's always been the case. I don't know who will object or call a meeting to discuss it, and I don't know how they will stop

> **INTEGRITY IS THE EQUIVALENT OF OXYGEN. WITHOUT IT A COMPANY SUFFOCATES AND DIES.**

it. But I can be absolutely certain that people will stand up and ask if this is now how we do business. A debate will ensue that I am confident will end in a unanimous rejection of the idea. No money will ever be bundled into a briefcase and handed to the buyer. Integrity is part of our minimum common denominator.

Just as they did with the multinational's kickback, I imagine that Semco's ethics watchdogs will emerge victorious. Outsiders will argue that I can't know this for certain, or that people may vote to pay the money in different circumstances. Yes, that could happen. But I am equally certain that the reaction would be intense enough that some people would threaten to quit and operations would be disrupted. So what's more valuable, paying a 10 percent kickback to win business or protecting the core of this company?

For me, the best part is that the owner of the company won't even participate in the debate. Integrity will develop without me precisely because of the minimum common denominator that we share at Semco. I'm not required to pen some lofty statement of values that any idiot can write. Shared values are those that evolve naturally over the years until one day you realize you're living by them.

SOMETIMES OUR OWN PEOPLE are at odds about which directions to take, and meetings of the mind don't occur. We're not advocating endless paralysis by analysis, nor striving to make a hippie commune out of our management team. Many times, leadership or initiative saves the day. And sometimes they create muddled outcomes, because encouraging people to act freely can lead to trouble—especially when there are no written or official guidelines.

Vicente Gomes, our technical assistance engineer, once cautioned his boss that the pumps we had delivered to the Belgian caustic soda giant, Carbocloro, would not work. His colleague, new engineer Valdomiro Costa, argued that the pumps would work fine after further tightening of their gaskets, the rubber rings that are attached to both ends of the pump.

The boss and Vicente insisted that this was not the solution, but Valdomiro persisted. He had experience and schooling the others didn't. He was so insistent that the three departed for the Carbocloro plant after a few days of technical disagreement.

Now, we were already famous at that particular plant because Rolney Magalhães, our sharply dressed sales manager, had once walked through the emergency showers without knowing that they would turn on as soon as someone pressed a switch with his foot. The workers all hid behind pumps and generators, racked with laughter at the sight of this "suit" in his drenched clothes.

Engineer Valdomiro and his colleagues showed up to solve the faulty pump problem. Valdomiro boldly grabbed a wrench and stepped up to the pump while the others retreated swiftly. Valdomiro looked behind his shoulder, snorted, and proceeded to crank. As soon as he did so, the pump emitted a long groan and exploded. Caustic soda blanketed the area like new fallen snow, while workers scattered in all directions.

Granted, this would never have happened in a company with established procedures, the very reason Carbocloro employees didn't dare tinker with the pump. But at Semco, our mission is clear: Make the customer's pumps work. All avenues are open, even if they lead to an embarrassing failure. We can only do this if we accept that absolute control over employees and how they conduct their jobs will ultimately hinder our business. Once we let go, the reward is that companies like Carbocloro remain steadfast customers, even after (or maybe because of) the entertaining shows we've performed at its plant.

INFORMATION IS POWER

Giving up control also means relinquishing exclusive rights to information. Privileged information is a dangerous source of power in any organization. Information that one person has that others lack can be terribly important, and can give them the upper hand.

To eliminate information hoarding and the illegitimate power it fosters, information must be shared. The argument that competitors might latch onto sensitive information if it is widely known is not persuasive enough to stop the free flow of information in my opinion.

Business information should be as useful and immediate as possible. Any good company is a moving target anyway. During the dot-com craze, everyone ran around with carefully constructed NDAs (nondisclosure agreements). One could end up in jail for talking in his sleep.

Certainly someone could conceivably draw conclusions about our strategy for products from our balance sheet, ads in the paper, and headhunting forays. So what? What can they do with that? Even if they received a copy of a highly confidential presentation on strategy, what can they glean? As I said, we start every new meeting as if the one before hadn't happened, and constantly reexamine everything. A two-week-old presentation may as well be last month's newspaper.

At any rate, all of our plans are limited to six months into the future. We deliberately project only half a year because of the assumptions people make—that information is right, so the plan must be right. But factors in the business world change so frequently that any plan can become obsolete. A five-year plan is ludicrous. We don't want to follow a structure that might become nonsense in six months. We brainstorm up to ten years into the future, but we only write down the next six months, a process that guarantees freedom. Besides, every one-year plan that I see has all the good things happening in the second half.

We would much rather look ahead just six months, since whatever looks bad on that horizon needs immediate action, not rhetoric. Doing so allows us to combine freedom with strong business sense—and they are not incompatible.

To be sure, openness, truth, and exposure can be as upsetting at Semco as anywhere else. I was reminded of that when I sent some very public e-mails about individual salaries. Even though we post our salaries at Semco, the e-mails angered people.

We don't use blind e-mail copies when we circulate information. If a sender copies his e-mail to others, everyone will see who the recipients are. Sometimes, people inadvertently copy an e-mail that contains a string of messages with upsetting comments. But if all communication is open, then it shouldn't be possible to "inadvertently" share information, right? Still, some topics are more sensitive than others are. Like salary talks.

This time, I sent everyone at Semco copies of an e-mail that contained details of particular salary negotiations. Jose Alignani, the CEO of our Cushman & Wakefield business, was infuriated, insisting I should be more delicate with this kind of communication. E-mails containing salary discussions can create all sorts of problems for unit managers, Jose reminded me. They're too direct, too easily misunderstood, and too hurtful. Some people are not ready for such open communication, he cautioned. People need time to adjust, and sometimes they have to adjust more than once.

Salaries are a sensitive subject, but open communication is important enough that it should be tested, even if there is a price to pay. It's at the very heart of a shared culture. If a discussion of salaries is taboo, what else is off limits? The only source of power in an organization is information, and withholding, filtering, or retaining information only serves those who want to accumulate power

THOSE WHO HOARD INFORMATION ARE ATTEMPTING TO ACCUMULATE POWER.

through hoarding. Once an e-mail is not circulated, or if it is edited, then illegitimate pockets of power are created. Some people are privy to information that others don't possess. Remove those pockets, and a company removes a source of dissatisfaction, bickering, and political feuding.

CUSTOMER CULTURE CLASH

Open communication and truth are not only factors when dealing with employees, they're equally important with clients.

It often takes a customer time to get used to Semco's way of doing business. Many of them are wary of our reputation for democracy, dissent, and flexibility. Those freedoms just mean chaos to people who don't appreciate them. While customers are not expected to adopt our philosophies when they hire us, we make our practices clear, and that has caused some unexpected culture clashes.

MY OWN PEOPLE HAVE often been flabbergasted at my admission of guilt for product deficiencies during customer presentations. Dismayed, they would see our case going down the drain. More often than not, however, the customer would be taken aback by my frankness, and believe in the rest of what we had to say.

In one famous incident, we'd been battling with Anglo

American Mines over who was at fault in a mishap with gold mixing equipment. I went to see them, and confessed that we had found drawings that definitively proved that the fault was ours. Though the drawings had been found some time before, I had only just learned about them.

Our people were shaken. The $450,000 cost of redoing the equipment was a lot to us at the time, but Anglo American reacted as I had hoped. They thanked us for our honesty, and ordered two more mixing machines. We used the money to fund the replacement of the older machines. They're our avid customers to this day.

On another occasion involving a presentation to a bank, I shared our findings about their engineering department with the directors seated around me. I said we should be hired because they had an incompetent engineering concept in place, and because their contracts were inflated, both of which indicated corruption to me. Everyone blanched. Jose Alignani glowered at me in the elevator down to the garage, as the rest of our group stared silently away. We received the contract, but Alignani and his people still spent the next two years explaining that I had not read the report carefully, and that I am a bit unpredictable. But after the bank's purchasing manager was fired for corruption in the second year, things improved.

My colleagues never know how I'm going to use internal information in front of a client, but neither do I. In the beginning, they didn't see the merit of being totally frank with the customer. They came to realize that this path is much more productive, although they are still afraid of where the conversation can go when they're not conducting it carefully.

On several occasions I have taken our internal profit calculations out of one of the director's briefcases and given the customer a copy. Here is what we plan to make as a profit, I've said. Do you think it's too much? What do you suggest? What should we do? Many times this is the first occasion in which a customer has seen a profit calculation, and he'll pinch himself. But this strategy almost always succeeds.

One time, I visited the director of another bank whose building we had just begun to manage. The property manager there had been known to sexually harass the cleaning women.

This man was close to some of the bank managers, and they protected him. I asked the director what he'd think if I brought him a newspaper clipping with the headline: "Bank Manager Harasses Women—Board Aware and Silent." He looked stunned, and our team members, not knowing that I would bring this up, looked at the ceiling, out the window, at their shoes.

After a brief pause, the bank director answered with two words: "Fire him." Since then, that bank has asked for our help with delicate issues that require meeting the truth head on.

LITTLE GUYS

At Semco, we practice truth with a simple formula: free sharing of information. We are so committed to it that we don't just tell people they have a right to information. We actively present it to them in e-mails and at democratic meetings. We also encourage people to learn how to use the information at their fingertips. It started because two decades ago Semco was run via a series of management meetings. I put the system in place, along with Clovis Bojikian and a handful of top managers, a group of us who came to be called the Musketeers. Every week the CEOs of each business unit would meet, and any interested party could attend.

In addition, once a month the top directors would meet. This monthly gathering centralized power in the directors' hands and was often the decisive moment for company plans. This closed group of directors became known as the Friends of the King. (No one knows where the moniker came from, but it stuck.)

The CEOs of the units, five at that time, had their own monthly meeting with their managers, and that gathering came to be called the Friends of the Prince. Every week, a third type of meeting took place that was open to all employees and was nicknamed the Little Guys Meeting.

Of course we also held quarterly board meetings with shareholders, and once a month an open meeting for all employees of each unit. The intention was to openly examine and debate Semco's numbers. Shop-floor workers, machinists, clerks, and cleaning people were invited to the open meeting.

The advantage of this system was that within a few days, information flowed to all levels, down to the humblest janitor. It was correct and honest information—not rumors or doctored reports and memos. Conversely, all worker concerns and suggestions flowed right back up.

In the mid-1980s and again in the early 1990s, a series of economic crises rocked Brazil. Few companies in developed nations have experienced such disastrous times. Semco's system of two-way communication made all the difference. We shared our director's concerns with employees at the Little Guys Meeting. They saw all the numbers and forecasts. They heard our worries. More often than not, the groups would break up to work together on solutions—which in those dark days involved layoffs. Ideas would flow upward; we'd receive new input, make suggestions, disagree, renew pressure, and start over. This always seems a drawn-out process to outsiders, and that creates the impression that crisis generates terror and prolonged suffering. But we never forget that we are dealing with adults who are responsible and well informed. They quickly offered solutions that were more clever and realistic than those first suggested by management. They also imagined radically different implementation. Once everyone had a chance to air their concerns, look at the figures, and share the pain of difficult decisions, the atmosphere became one of trust and transparency. The dull rage that comes from layoffs or cost cutting was directed at the economy, or particular management, but not at the company as a whole.

This probably explains why we never had negative press during the crises, never suffered collective lawsuits from employees, and never faced a strike in more than fifteen years of adjusting to the difficult Brazilian economy. This is certainly not the story told by our industry peers. All have been plagued by huge lawsuits from ex-employees, obstruction by Brazil's strong unions, and incessant press investigation.

Naturally, no matter how much we grow or how well we do, we still occasionally confront unexpected losses of contracts to competitors and deal with sudden downturns in the economy. It's vital that we have a system that adjusts organically to these ups and downs.

Given all that, we quickly realized that opening our books to employees meant they had to read them, which required training. Complicated accounting procedures don't make much sense to the common man.

For example, profit-and-loss statements report revenue and then separately subtract variable and fixed costs. As such, you are unable to identify the payroll, for example. Payroll is divided up into various line items, such as selling and general administrative costs, manufacturing overhead or services provided, and is then further broken up between nominal salaries and benefits, social security, and so forth. It doesn't exist as a separate expense.

Confusing.

To our straight-arrow shop-floor workers, these convoluted reports just clouded the issues. They were right. We needed a clearer method of presenting our accounts. We realized there were only a half dozen numbers that really mattered at any of our businesses (a fact I've found to be true of all businesses I've encountered in the last twenty years).

Once we created a new, simpler accounting system, we needed to validate it. So we turned to the one organization that could establish its credibility. After all, factory workers tend to see David Copperfield when they look at accountants. We didn't want them believing we'd simplified our numbers to the extent that they didn't add up, or contradicted our more complex accounts. Who could validate this new process for the workers?

The union could. We met with Walter Barelli, an economist who has served as Brazil's secretary of labor. At the time he lead the Inter-Union Department for the Study of Economics and Statistics, making him the all-powerful czar of a socialist worker's view of capital.

Mr. Barelli and his staff were stunned to hear that any businessperson wanted to open company books to workers, not to mention to a Socialist union. So, pinching themselves periodically, they sat with us for long hours over many weeks to design a simple but truthful profit-and-loss statement. They also accepted our invitation to come to the company regularly and teach workers how to read balance sheets. Their lessons led to a Semco instruction guide illustrated with cartoon drawings, in keeping with our tradition of taking things lightly. The drawings equated a company to a supermarket, with workers on both sides of the counter, buying and selling. It moved from there into the revenue stream, how the payroll is made up, and so forth. Using the booklet, the union held many classes, and our people filled the meeting rooms to learn. Soon after, the monthly meetings to report on and debate our accounts became very lively indeed.

We were convinced that employees who knew the whole truth could be counted on to stay longer, better understand the vagaries of economics, improve their work life, and thus enrich our financial performance. After all, they had an important profit-sharing program to make them part of the gains.

Workers have benefited greatly from the new accounting information. They are able to make better decisions about their own salaries and financial planning. When communication is open, employees understand our books and pay close attention to them. They're not just improving their own chances of making more money, they're improving Semco's as well.

This is why the culture that arises from daily acts takes the place of corporate policies. Instead of writing ourselves down in a set of rules, we evolve slowly based on what we do.

But evolution can be quite painful.

I once adamantly believed that more than one of our manufacturing plants had to close. Our business was becoming increasingly global; and when I pondered the future, I saw imports devastating a local manufacturing industry that concentrated on producing everything in Brazil. I believed we could outsource much more than we did, thus removing the burden of our existing legacy. It would make us lighter on our feet, and freer to move into new formats. I called a meeting, and most of the executives came. I laid out my concerns and my plan, and they were shocked. You cannot be right, they exclaimed. So we studied further. Over the next few weeks I called several meetings. A few people showed up out of pity for me, the rest refused to spend time on such an absurd assumption. Eventually it became clear that no one would show up at these meetings anymore, so I gave up.

Almost a full year later these same executives reconvened to debate the plan. Some of them had let the idea mature and finally thought there was some merit in it, even though they didn't believe in my particular proposal. More meetings ensued, and they showed up for these, eventually putting into place a plan that bore some resemblance to my theory.

You will say that the company would have been better off had I insisted on my way and saved Semco twelve months of expenses by closing the plants. But the plan was refined greatly in everyone's mind during that one year, and the end solution was an improvement. Also, a lot of people were confident of the direction that we needed to take, so were infinitely more convincing when dealing with the employees, clients, and unions.

In the end, it's an exchange that works: Out go mission statements, credos, and the control they exert; and in come self-interest, principles arising from practice, and a developing set of values. As control wanes, creativity and shared values bloom. An army that fights for what it believes in arises from this harvest of ideas, varied practices, and close contact with the real world. Missions take a backseat in the army jeep, and generals can relax while the soldiers and lieutenants draw the map.

DOING NOTHING

Dissent and democracy go hand in hand. It's also good management technique. What traditional executives don't consider is that decisions arising from debate are implemented much more quickly because explanations, alternatives, objections, and uncertainties have already been aired. As a result of democracy, employees have had their say, and projects or ideas have been analyzed from every point of view.

And that means tolerating and even encouraging dissent, which at times isn't exactly as pleasant as a stroll on the beach. I found that out in a long-running soap opera involving an employee, whose name I'll change to Yolanda, who had been dismissed from one job only to move into another on the same floor. She made it clear she was unhappy about her new situation, and tension began to mount between her and her director of operations at Semco Johnson Controls. He could have simply fired her, but he was wary of the consequences. For one, there'd be a lot of explaining to do to other employees. He also wanted to be careful not to allow his personal dislike for her to affect their relationship. Firing her wouldn't be fair and would have been fairly messy.

Yolanda believed she'd been relegated to Johnson Controls because she'd complained about her previous job, even though she was convinced that her dissatisfaction was legitimate.

Yolanda was convinced that she was being given more difficult work than anyone else, in an effort to manipulate her into resigning. She couldn't prove anything, of course, since maneuvering of that kind is inherently subtle. She increased the volume of her complaints, hoping others would back her up, or protect her somehow. After all, she'd been with the company a long time, and had helped start up the Semco Foundation, which strives to implement Semco practices in educational institutions. But the brass on her floor was also close to her boss, and did nothing out of respect for letting the process play out.

As the situation worsened, several directors favored firing Yolanda immediately; others thought we should phase her out. Many were indignant that such a person was left unchecked by top management; some supported her dissent but thought she was defeating her own point by voicing her insults on the office floor instead of to the targets of her ire.

There was pressure for a formal Semco reaction, but we could only respond one way: If she wanted to quit, that was up to her, but we could not fire her for dissent. We'd always said dissent was important to us, and Yolanda was putting us to the test. Our integrity was at stake, too. All the brickbats and barbs from Yolanda were less damaging to morale than firing her for dissent would have been. Later, when someone else has complaints, they will know they have the right to speak out.

So we did what we always do when there is dissent: nothing. We believe blindly in the virtues of dissent. We don't want a crowd of brainwashed workers. We don't want them to sing company songs, memorize company mission statements, and learn to speak only when spoken to.

Sure, it was hard, but it was up to the people who worked around Yolanda to resolve the issues behind the complaints. The people at Semco are responsible and sensitive adults who know how to judge such outbursts. And if she was right, we'd all learn something and change.

Another business unit could have hired Yolanda. After all,

a person can be right for one job and a disaster in another. But then her boss chose to lobby for her transfer to another unit. She went to Cushman & Wakefield Semco, but that didn't improve her low opinion of the company directors, whom she continued to criticize openly. By this time, it was obvious that years of secretarial work had taken its toll on Yolanda, who thought she deserved a more challenging position. A mix of the Peter Principle and what may have been a perfectly legitimate aspiration—who could know?

This happened in 1999. Yolanda is still with us at Cushman & Wakefield Semco and has settled down. Her griping eventually subsided and then stopped. She now handles relatively complex tasks with the help of assistants; it seems to be a reasonable, working compromise. It's still hard to say how happy she is, but she smiles a lot more. Some years ago she recommended Semco to her twenty-three-year-old daughter, Valeria, who now works for ERM. To date, I don't know what changed in her. Could I have found out, by requesting information or talking to her in the corridor? Maybe. But could I have done that and not gotten involved? Process is king, I believe, and so these things have to play themselves out; there's no right answer.

Sure, it takes some organizational cold-bloodedness, and it might leave the reader, as well as many Semco employees, miffed or unconvinced. That, however, is the price for giving up policies, procedures, missions, and credos. Just as our aversion to long-term analysis is based on the realization that it can be a waste of time and energy to attempt to foresee every possible twist and turn of the road ahead, finding the root cause of every problem can also be unproductive. She was once a pain in the neck, now she isn't. Case closed. Time to move on. Perhaps when Yolanda retires from Semco in a few years, we still won't know what really went on.

Since I opened this chapter dealing with the paradox of profit coexisting with the notions of mission and credo, I'll close with another for the sake of symmetry. Maybe you don't want to know. Because the more you know the less you understand.

- **Why not admit that you screwed up?**

- **Why bother going to the trouble of finding out what went wrong?**

- **Why are financial reports impossible to decipher?**

SEVEN

FRIDAY

- Hang out with strangers, weirdos, and misfits.
- Hire a new boss.
- Shut down a factory.

MANY COMPANIES RELAX THEIR dress codes on Friday, and good for them. At Semco, we tore up the dress code for the entire seven-day weekend. It's a simple, powerful step toward creating an organization that has evolved from a collection of rigidly segregated occupational specialties to a rich blend of diverse skills, attitudes, and personalities.

Once upon a time, it was easy to caricature the idiosyncrasies of various tribes in the manufacturing industry. People lived up to the clichés. Engineers went around with plastic, shirt-pocket protectors for their colored pens. The marketing people wore loud yellow shirts and piped music into their section, while the controllers favored thick glasses and carried oversized brief cases. The owner drove a Mercedes. The janitors owned old Ford Galaxys. Salesmen sported worn shoes and cars and looked as if they'd just gotten back from a Willy Loman conference.

Like talent, anthropology in the workplace often goes unnoticed. This may be because tribalism now looks a bit different on the surface. Plastic pen protectors are out of style and on casual days, everyone looks alike in the parking lot.

Tribes, however, often speak a language that outsiders can't understand. If you try talking shop with tax attorneys or information technology types, you won't understand any more than if they were teenage hip-hop rappers.

Tribalism satisfies the human need to belong. Tribes have all sorts of rituals designed to exclude outsiders, include members, test loyalty, and reinforce belonging. The challenge is to foster integration by mixing people of different backgrounds, experiences, and ages in working groups and office setups. We've done that at Semco in our offices. Our employees work at a different desk every day, sitting next to a different person who might be younger or older and who may have a wildly different background than the person who sat there the day before.

We've done it in our garden meetings, where blue- and white-collar workers rub elbows in the same outdoor space, and we've done it with programs that encourage workers to move around the company, seek new challenges, and test the limits of their interests and abilities.

As people begin to realize that job rotation is about exploring new worlds and fighting repetition and boredom, the concept catches on quickly. Once tribe members begin to circulate, any departmental mind-set is quickly undermined, and uniformity is left behind. People don't have to look alike or work alike. Pretty soon, units will include workers who can speak for or defend another unit because they've visited or worked in that other place themselves. They understand it, even if they are not similar to the others.

SALT AND PEPPER, SWEET AND SOUR

As an avid cook and music buff, I've learned that stew (say a *boeuf bourguignon*) parallels Ravel's *Bolero*. They both seem so easy. Stew apparently has to sit just long enough for the meat to tenderize, and *Bolero* seems like an unending succession of the same simple notes. Like a company culture, they both belie the complexity, timing, and fragile combination that contribute to success. If you add too much salt too early in the stew, or make the flame too high, nothing will save the dish in a few hours time. Conductors, also, can easily miscalculate by playing *Bolero* in front of sophisticated audiences. One mistake in the intensity or timing, and the piece climaxes too soon, making the ending a mess by rushing through the last few minutes.

Culture in an organization is similar. If there are too many MBAs, it tastes salty. By drawing students from the same social strata, subjecting them to the same system of rewards and punishment, and immersing them in the same theories, attitudes, prejudices, and practices, graduate schools of business produce an astounding level of uniformity among MBA recipients, a uniformity that is a danger to an organization. Change—never easy—is made more difficult by literally walling off viable alternatives that do not have the orthodox MBA seal of approval. Weighed down with an allegiance to the past, organizations lose their flexibility. They stagnate.

Companies respect conformity and uniformity, but they fail to see how limiting both are. Without change and innovation, companies cannot adapt to new realities. At one time, Singer was one of the biggest companies in the United States. Today, we're not using Singer cell phones because the company was unable to adapt.

When young people or seasoned managers come to us from completely different worlds, we try to value the differences they bring, to find merit and charm in the new ingredients.

Jonathan Graicar is a good example. A handsome blond with city smarts, he always wears designer clothes and is at ease in any cappuccino bar or disco. He is fast with numbers and anxious to make a million or two (after all, he's already nineteen), much like other similar-looking and similar-aged whiz kids at Semco. He cannot possibly imagine doing the same thing for two consecutive weeks, much less thirty years. Jonathan is the secretary of a group that set itself up to detonate what they view as Semco's complacent culture! They meet every two weeks to think up ways of injecting new life into Semco's products and services. They're the ones who, for reasons unknown to us straight-laced folks, think that Semco will only be a success when we become a $1 billion company. The rest of us shrug and avoid their meetings.

Most of the time, Jonathan sits near João Vendramim, who at age sixty-one has been with us for twenty years and is our in-house philosopher. João uses computers, but likes to prop a pencil behind his ear. When they first met, he figured he needed to explain to Jonathan what a pencil was for.

Cultural integration trumps cultural preservation. Even at Semco, people tend to explain that certain things are done in a certain way, a reminder that preserving the culture that evolves in an organization is just as dangerous as ignoring it, as communities like the Amish or Orthodox Jewish sects have found. Only certain people can live under such severe rules and with such limited options. When tribes coexist in a workplace, they impart to each other new concepts and different experiences. They form their flavor slowly.

Diversity, however, can throw together leaders and followers whose styles are almost incompatible. Felipe Knudsen, a manager of our Bidcom unit, discovered this himself. Knudsen had a rather high opinion of himself, one that might befit a manager at another company, but that was out of place at Semco. He wielded his power too overtly for our democratic environment, riding roughshod over minority opinions and leaving the more important tasks to himself. He also had a penchant for yellow ties. It happened that the bathroom doors near his office were adorned with a Barbie doll and a Bob-the-Builder doll instead of signs indicating which gender should enter. Some of Knudsen's employees took it upon themselves to put together another doll—a Bob wearing Barbie clothes and a yellow tie. They hung the doll exactly between the two bathroom doors. Their message was plain: The high and mighty manager could pick and choose whichever bathroom he wanted, and the other men and women would just make way. Knudsen saw the humor in the stunt, and the Bob doll with the yellow tie hung on the wall for months. His colleagues think it helped him slip into the Semco rhythm. It put management's proper role into perspective for Knudsen, and afterward he was less assertive. Knudsen's style still differs from other Bidcom workers, but it didn't matter after they made it clear that diversity was a plus, not something to be flattened by a top-heavy tractor.

Diversity is more than a politically correct buzzword. There's a place for everyone at Semco, including those who are not impressed or in any other way moved by the Semco system. And there is also a place for those who find that a job is nothing but a job, and participation imposes a weight they'd rather not carry. Even those kinds of people are welcome because our culture finds them valuable. They teach us important lessons— e.g., how to listen, compromise, and communicate, and how to be patient, tolerant, and resilient. By making a place for the oddballs, the malcontents, and the incompatible, we accept the consequences, both positive and negative. Things may not go as smoothly or as fast, but maybe slowing down will let us catch our breath and see new opportunities instead of the usual blur.

A GAME OF CHESS

That brings up the question of how we hire or add new people to our tribe. We do this by respecting tribal rites of passage that are central to the evaluation and selection of new members.

This priority was evident in the spring of 2001, when we decided to hire a finance controller for the corporate staff. The business was expanding rapidly and we needed a strong liaison with our American partners like Cushman & Wakefield.

Advertisements with Semco's name at the top ran in several newspapers asking for résumés via e-mail. Four hundred people replied. There were no rules for narrowing down the respondents. We didn't want a list of requirements to limit our options, so the idea was to make the process highly intuitive and to follow our gut reactions. I liken the approach to the way a chess grandmaster uses intuition and analytical skills to see a board. Bearing in mind that, as Clovis says, a person's curriculum vitae is advertising and therefore rarely includes honest assessments of shortcomings, we promptly made a lot of mistakes about whom to call for an interview. Great candidates surely slipped through our fingers, and many others should have.

Clovis and I, joined by a small group of senior executives, winnowed the pile down to the twenty candidates that each of us classified A+.

The twenty were invited to participate in a collective interview, which we sometimes use as a rodeo of sorts. The candidates have an opportunity to see their rivals face-to-face, meet a cross section of Semco people and, regardless of their stellar résumés, show us how they handle pressure and the dynamics of personal interaction. Four at a time came to these meetings with nearly forty Semco employees, who collectively interviewed the entire field of candidates. It's a great way to show an outsider what life is like inside Semco, introduce them to our freewheeling style, and, frankly, scare them off if the chemistry isn't right.

Our interview and selection process was not unlike the way we hire at every level. We rely heavily on the shock value of intensive mutual exposure. The candidates can decline, of course, and there's no penalty. They can continue with a more private interview process, but we believe that only by spending a lot of time with the greatest number of employees, will a candidate get any real sense of Semco. At the same time, Semco employees get to voice an opinion about the people who might be joining their team. With this overwhelming and admittedly daunting exposure, we address compatibility head on.

COLLECTIVE JOB INTERVIEWS BUILD CONSENSUS AND HELP AVOID SURPRISES.

However, before the collective interviews begin, we create a template for the job. This is a draft list of the qualities sought, along with numerical weightings that should be attached to each of these. Employees help design the template. They can log on to the company intranet and suggest the qualities and qualifications that we should look for in a candidate, and then assign scoring points to each attribute. Basic qualifications, like international experience or schooling, fluent English, and a firm command of financial technique, are not a part of the template.

These basics are either irrelevant, or they're a prerequisite covered by testing. For example, if English is vital, as it was in this case, the finalists take a test called Test of English as a Foreign Language, Business Version. It evaluates the candidate's ability to communicate well for business purposes. An intricate test of financial knowledge gives the candidates two hours to put together a balance sheet, comment on profit-and-loss statements, and answer questions about tax laws and current issues in finance.

As basic abilities, therefore, English or finance skills shouldn't have any weight attached to them, which meant that an MBA from Wharton, or wherever, would do nothing for an applicant's grading. This is important because it prevents placing undue value on experience and schooling. The fact that a candidate has an MBA is worthless to the template. Those skills may open the door for a candidate, but they add little to his qualifications, so we don't review or grade those basic abilities. While it may have gotten the candidate in the door, the master's degree doesn't give him a better chance of landing the job.

That sounds counterproductive but, in fact, it's not. If we included an MBA credential in the template, we'd end up with a raft of MBA candidates and that leads straight to what I was complaining about a few pages ago—uniformity.

The qualities listed on the template for this job included a quick analytical mind, the capacity to integrate easily, an attitude of teamwork, transparency and openness, an independent attitude, a career of deliberate and solid growth, and a sense of humor.

Interviewers rate candidates on a scale of one to ten. Of the ten possible points, two go to the interviewer's feeling as to whether this is the right person for the job.

After a template is designed, two or three interested Semco workers volunteer to coordinate the interview process. Someone calls all the candidates and asks them if they'll come. The date of the collective interview is then posted so any employee who is interested can participate. For the first round of controller interviews, thirty-seven Semco employees responded, which reflected the importance of this new position.

By the same token, if no one had shown up for the collective interview, then we'd have eliminated the controller's position before it was even filled because it would have demonstrated that no one at the company cared about it.

The twenty candidates were reduced to nine. Then, the thirty-seven Semco interviewers were handed a copy of the template showing which attributes were important and the score value assigned to each. They could then show up for the next rounds of interviews and ask whatever questions they wanted, in any language, in search of answers for the template.

Each candidate made three to five trips to Semco, spending an hour or two with different groups, and having contact with more Semco people than they could possibly remember. A dozen Semco employees showed up for the final round of interviews with the three best candidates.

These sessions were intense but as lighthearted as we could make them because everyone tried to reduce the stress the process put on the candidate. We were ganging up on them, after all.

One finalist was particularly self-confident, fluent in many languages, and was not at all reluctant to speak highly of himself. One interviewer couldn't let that pass without a comment, and he inquired in a gentle and nonconfrontational manner, "Did anyone ever tell you that you are very arrogant?"

Unfazed, the candidate said that it wasn't the first time he had heard that but although he seemed arrogant at first sight, people who had worked with and for him would tell us that this impression disappeared over time. His reply earned him many supporters, although others believed it was a studied response to a substantial fault.

The three finalists were seen one after the other on the same day. Some of the dozen or so Semco interviewers had seen them before, but most had not. Each Semco participant then filled out his template response sheet. The resulting scores would determine the winner. Their rankings would be unknown to the

CFO of Cushman & Wakefield, who would also interview each of the three. If the results differed, the Semco group would reconvene to hear the Cushman & Wakefield CFO's arguments. They could change or stand by their ratings. Whatever they decided, it would overrule Cushman & Wakefield's CFO.

Incidentally, my vote was subordinate to the Semco employees' choice, too. My opinion would be factored in the same way as the CFO of Cushman & Wakefield.

As it turned out, the candidate who got the job was chosen by virtual consensus. Ivan Maluf impressed Semco by being both a careful listener and a man full of firm opinions. He had neither an MBA nor a finance background, but he'd been CFO for Philips and a GE Capital company and scored extremely well on our technical test. In one interview, I asked him why he was unemployed.

He'd left the GE Capital company four months before when they decided to pull out of Brazil. He had turned off the lights, received a bonus, and entertained several offers to move to other GE companies. Instead, he used the bonus to search carefully for a job and had refused three final offers from other companies.

What we liked about him was that between gigs he wasn't just spending all the time job hunting. He filled his days with his other interest, storytelling. Of Arab descent, he volunteered for a Jewish congregation in a program that sent people to shantytowns to tell stories to poor children. He'd even taken courses to develop this ability. While he told stories and looked for work, his wife's income as a headhunter and his bonus from GE kept his household together.

Several months after he started, we began receiving e-mails full of praise for Ivan. Fran Clerkin, CFO of Cushman & Wakefield International, lauded Ivan as beyond everyone's wildest dreams.

As unusual as our hiring practices sound, it's actually traditional corporations that rely on loony recruiting methods, like letting HR handle it or moving people into jobs without first exposing them to the people they'll be working with. They're using a hundred-year-old system to choose their people while we respect a time-honored, hundred-thousand-year-old method of admitting members to the tribe. Cavemen and fellows in medieval artisan guilds worked no differently. They all based decisions on a newcomer's acceptance by an established group.

Our collective interviews allow candidates to see that thirty-seven people are interested in the person who fills the job vacancy. They can hear their concerns, their preferences, even their complaints. Some applicants run screaming for the hills, but it's better for both sides to understand what's required at the very beginning. At Semco, we don't want to spend six months trying to integrate a new hire only to discover there is no chance of compatibility.

At Semco, we never intentionally misrepresent the company in conversations with potential employees. It makes no sense to be less than candid. And with thirty-seven interviewers, there's an extra informal, unplanned, and uncontrolled element to the process that adds to the chance that one of those people will say something close to the bone and revealing, either in jest or between the lines. Job candidates can form valuable impressions from side comments and attitudes, and they can glean a lot of information over the course of five or six rounds of interviews.

On the one hand, we unmask the inscrutable face of the company. On the other, we create something of a free-for-all that leaves us vulnerable and that sometimes is highly effective at persuading candidates that they might be happier elsewhere.

By the end, candidates have a strong sense of their compatibility and of the balance between their personal goals and ours. Ivan came back six times, and when he was finally hired, he knew several people by name that I myself had never met. Consequently, when the successful candidate shows up for his first day of work, there are people on hand who are already known to him, with whom he feels a bond, people who want him on the team and are ready to support his success. The benefits of our hiring process thus outlive the interview and selection period. It may take longer to hire a candidate, but productivity and sustainability make up grandly for any lost time.

MIXING OIL AND WATER

Another thing we often do is let members of one group check out the jobs of another. Our very first tribe integration program took place many years ago, when we put a small group of finance executives together with salespeople. At the time, the debate concerned the salesmen's propensity to sell at any cost, thereby eating up the company's working capital with overgenerous payment terms. The debate raged but never went anywhere. When we proposed that a finance specialist and one salesman change places, many people were flabbergasted. They told us that salesmen and accountants don't mix and are not interchangeable. They warned that the salesman's customers would be dismayed and hostile, and that we'd lose business. Further, they thought the salesman was sure to make serious errors while in the finance office.

We did it anyway, and new worlds opened up.

From finance, we chose a short, stout, hardheaded cost accountant named Antonio Carlos Iotti. He wore extra thick glasses with a definite greenish sheen. He smirked a lot, making it impossible to know whether he was being humorous or smug. He habitually nodded as others spoke, so people always believed that he was in wholehearted agreement with them. As soon as they finished, he'd nod again, and then declare, "I disagree entirely."

Antonio belonged to the tribe of long-lost, eccentric accounting savages, five men, who had joined Semco at almost the same time. All had worked for an offbeat Italian entrepreneur who made industrial sewing machines, and where business was often conducted at the top of the Italian's lungs.

At Semco, Iotti rose to plant controller. He was known for his passionate attention to detail and his immense work capacity. He was tough, and he directly challenged many operational assumptions. On some days he left work at midnight after finishing a calculation in his small, exact handwriting with his face glued to the paper and his tiny, swollen hands pressing on a pencil. He was wary of computers, but the man could calculate in his head like there was no tomorrow, and no one ever caught him making a mistake. Most of all, he was deeply suspicious of salesmen.

So we put him in charge of sales, and for a year he went out to see the real world. A typical desk man, he had a hard time finding the addresses he was now obliged to visit. Very quickly, he revised his ideas about salespeople and their let's-make-a-deal attitude, and about the ease of selling on stricter credit plans. Slowly, he began to take a different and more sympathetic view of the wide world of sales, and he soon became the CEO of that manufacturing unit.

The most direct result was that the finance people never again confronted the sales group with simplistic requests for shorter payment terms. The two tribes now empathize with each other, and they're more careful about plans that involve the other.

It's not a perfect world. We know that some strife among different groups will occur. But we're willing to accept that and open ourselves to diversity, unlike most other workplaces. We've found that the advantages outweigh the disadvantages. Cliques, sects, and clubs that reinforce tribal

> STRANGE AND SEEMINGLY INCOMPATIBLE COMBINATIONS CAN YIELD POWERFUL RESULTS.

affiliations in harmful ways can be easily dismantled when employees manage themselves. What's more, the overall tribal-bonding mechanism loses traction. In an open organization like Semco, people spend less time in the office and have more time to themselves. Their need to belong to a tribe can be satisfied with hobbies or in community activities and doesn't have to be met in the office.

The assumption that the workplace is where tribal connections are made because most waking hours are spent there wouldn't hold true if people were free to mingle work and personal time in a looser way, as they can with a seven-day weekend. The payoff is that the various groups show immense respect for each other. In our operation, departmental biases and deprecating comments about other groups are practically nonexistent. This relatively smooth integration extends to our newest members, the refugees of the dot-com bust.

Most traditonal business organizations would probably gag at the thought of adopting jobless orphans accustomed to pulling all-nighters, working from a bean bag chair or bringing their dogs and pet ferrets to the office. They'd be written off as too flakey, too disruptive, too out of control.

And that's precisely why they are candidates for membership in our tribal federation. We want to blend their talent reservoir with ours. The dot-com kids didn't fail, the system failed them. Instead of creating a sustainable mix—the rule makers with the rule breakers, the dreamers joined to the hardheaded doers, and the revolutionaries married to the reactionaries—

Dad handed over the car keys and credit card to Junior and turned his back.

In the organization of the future, there has to be a place for the talents of these dot-commers, and for the thousands who come into the job market at twenty-two or even eighteen, since most of the world's teenagers never attend college. Businesses must be structured with them in mind, so the new views, wide-eyed curiosity, and start-up skills they brought to their own enterprises can be utilized. At that point, the mature veterans can step in and offer some "adult" perspective. Without recognizing this, many traditional companies will face the same fate as some of the industrial giants of the twentieth century like Singer Sewing Machines, International Harvester, Westinghouse, RCA, and Woolworth & Co. In the middle of the twentieth century, these companies were indomitable. No one could imagine a time when they wouldn't exist as a huge part of the economy. Now they're mere shadows of their former selves, if they exist at all. Traditional companies today face the same dilemma. They may look good for a time and convince Wall Street that the current quarter is glowing, but without new ideas, new approaches, and new blood, they won't last either.

A sustainable company wouldn't hesitate to put a fifty-seven-year-old GM alumni in an office with a former Silicon Valley whiz kid. Both with equal freedom to pursue their passions, both with significant talents to offer. The twenty-five-year-old would not be subject to the fifty-seven-year-old's rules, but would be eager to tap his wisdom and learn from his experience. In exchange, the elder worker wouldn't restrain, but rather recognize that new talent and entrepreneurial spirit are hallmarks of successful organizations.

As tribes mix, a constantly evolving culture emerges. It becomes evident that profound respect for differences, idiosyncrasies, and democratic ideals produces a new kind of organization, where people know there's a place for self-management, self-propulsion, and self-discipline. All of Semco's business units consistently perform above published parameters of productivity per employee because efficiency is unleashed when workers can repeatedly dive into their reservoirs of talent. Loosening up and rejecting the military model unleashes productivity. I believe this, and our numbers back it up.

It's easy to talk about respecting diversity, tribal characteristics, and dissent; but anyone who has tried to lead in a democratic manner knows that it can be frustrating, slow, and cumbersome. That's why business leaders often simply command and lead, taking the short route, with little concern for their employees or their customers. This kind of business model is a path to nowhere; it doesn't lead to the productivity gains that occur when people find it worthwhile and even inspiring to get up in the morning for work.

A coq au vin cannot be compared to Chicken McNuggets—even if both are merely cooked fowl. Taking the long way, simmering a slow stew of culture, tribalism, and democracy, serves up a far more savory dish.

Organizations mistakenly believe that productivity can always be raised. Productivity stagnates or falls when workers are waiting for someone to tell them what to do, or when they're following a formal plan, or confining themselves to the dictates of their job descriptions.

At Semco, self-organized employee groups have discovered that they can harness extra productivity by eliminating the immense daily waste of time lost to unclear goals, adolescent-style rules, infighting and gossip, even traffic jams.

In our inventory business, every time our teams are about to begin a new inventory, they spend half an hour bantering about the best way to do the job. They've done many inventories using the newest computer equipment, and there's an established system to it, but they still always look for improvements.

Marcio Batoni dreaded the idea that Brazil might make it to the World Cup soccer final. Although a fan of Ronaldo (this generation's Pele) and his team of magicians, he was worried about an enormous inventory scheduled for a new customer on the same day. Carrefour, the largest supermarket chain in Brazil, had recently hired Semco RGIS, and as luck would have it, had chosen the worst possible day to take inventory at forty-two hypermarkets in more than twenty cities. They'd scheduled it for June 30, the day of the World Cup finals.

On a typical day, Semco RGIS has a 5 to 10 percent absentee rate, mostly because people have difficulty reaching some of the inventory sites. Batoni knew that between 30 and 40 percent of his staff wouldn't show up for work if Brazil won the World Cup and the country took to the streets to celebrate. In most countries, it's just the team that plays in a championship. In Brazil, the entire nation takes to the field.

Of course Brazil won, and Sunday turned into an all-day celebration. Sheer havoc reigned in every city. Even a command-and-execute organization would have had a hard time convincing Brazilians to show up for work that day. We needed more than a thousand workers at once, and even Semco RGIS didn't have that many people. We'd been counting on a worker's co-operative and several independent contractors to pull off this complex logistical nightmare.

In the traditional corporate model, Batoni would have issued threats and unleashed a reign of terror to coerce workers to show up. But as you know, that's not how we work.

Managers and employees throughout the country asked workers to give their word they'd turn up for the inventory, regardless of how the Cup turned out. That Sunday, each unit managed itself, deciding themselves how to work around the Cup. Some people began their inventory early, and took a two-hour break for the game. Others jumped in their cars fifteen minutes before the game was over. Our profit margin was a negligible 1.2 percent below budget, which meant that our unit leaders hadn't used bonuses or overtime as incentive to show up. Self-management prevailed at a time when a traditional carrot-and-stick approach would surely have meant poorer results. In fact, the second largest supermarket chain in Brazil asked us to step in and replace our major competitor only a week after the World Cup, when our competitor failed to put together enough people to count inventory at sixty smaller stores.

In the end, self-management won the day. People all over the country understood what the Carrefour account meant to Semco RGIS. As usual, the numbers were on the table, and our plans had been openly discussed. It was no longer management's nightmare. We've learned that when people don't understand their role and don't grasp the purpose of a process, then the group only uses 70 or 80 percent of its talent and expertise. It squanders the amount that's locked up until people dip into their reservoir of talent, but they'll dip in only in an environment that encourages them to do so.

Our first experience with self-management came in the 1980s, when we needed to move into a bigger factory. On several different days, nearly all of Semco's employees filed onto buses and visited several potential locations. They eventually chose the site that upper management liked least, but we stuck to our commitment to democracy and self-management, and went along with their choice.

Since then, we've allowed employees to choose how to spend year-end money on things like company parties, presents for children, or home party baskets. Workers make middle management decisions like allocating money to refurbish the cafeteria. Our workers also decided to ensure that two employees sit on the company board and participate when a plant closure or layoff plan is discussed.

The antithesis of a long-simmering stew of self-management is the shake 'n' bake–style of management epitomized by the military, an extremely tribal institution. Some years ago, after having been named Brazilian Businessman of the Year, I spoke to the Joint Chiefs of Staff of Brazil and the Supreme War College. Hundreds of senior military officers, including generals, admirals, and brigadiers, filled the room. There were so many polished buttons, starched uniforms, and rows of shiny medals that I shuddered to think how many orderlies awoke at five that morning with flannel cloths and steaming irons in their hands.

I'd spoken against army rule at massive rallies since my university days, when Brazil was a military dictatorship. For years I'd written critiques of the military in Brazil's main daily newspaper. Surely everyone in my audience knew that I was not exactly enamored with their view of the world.

After some remarks about Brazil as a whole, I dived into the issue of hierarchy and organizational rule. Some forty minutes later, three of the officers left. Before the question-and-answer session, we lost another few dozen star-studded uniforms. Then the real debate began. The remaining officers unanimously believed that where there is no clear order, there is only confusion, which leads to disobedience and chaos. In other words, they thought that if people are left to their own devices, they will have no sense of direction and turn into an undisciplined mass. I can't say that I changed any opinions that day, but I did give them something to think about.

I've heard this same line of thought hundreds of times over the years, in talks with leaders from all walks of life. Speaking to a group of executives at MIT's Sloan Fellows Program in late 2001, I encountered the same incredulity about self-management that I had heard from the Brazilian military leaders. One participant, a highly placed colonel in Singapore's government, wanted to talk about breaking unions. He asked whether Margaret Thatcher's philosophy of iron rule wasn't the best approach.

Yes, I answered, if you want to break unions, then force is a good tactic to employ. If you recognize, however, that labor unions play a vital role, your strategy will change.

In most conventional organizations, major decisions are only made by top-level managers. Everyone else is invited to check their brains at the door. That kind of management style can produce hostile and extremist views among workers. Combined with drastic formulations like Jack Welch's mantra to fire the bottom 10 percent every year, such an approach crushes morale and instills an us-versus-them mentality that leads to a reign of terror on both sides. The workers say, "We could care less if the company goes belly up, and good riddance." Management replies, "It's a cold cruel world out there, and we may just have to leave you for dead and say *hasta la vista*, baby."

Is that bad for business, or what?

Jack Welch himself is a tremendous example of personal and corporate success, except that his form of leadership does not necessarily create sustainability. GE may or may not continue to prosper; I'm betting that its glory days are over. In the long run, a sustainable organization is better than a charismatic central figure. Rarely do the two coincide.

Most managers rarely stop to think twice about military-inspired policies or the confrontational, command-and-control strategies that seem to work so well. Although such strategies are thought to be efficient, they're usually destructive. Such tactics often play to the personal insecurities of board members and shareholders, or pit one group of employees against another. Unfortunately, they only result in a show of force—and applause from Wall Street—rather than meaningful solutions to real problems.

If humans are organized in a huge, complex group, they need complex regulations and procedures to govern them. If their organization is simplified, the way they're managed can be simplified, too. Best of all, they can manage themselves. If you want to know what time each of forty thousand employees arrive in the morning, you'll need a complex system of time clocks, cameras, penalties, and rewards. If you organize employees into groups of ten people each following a customized seven-day weekend, those clusters can be counted on to monitor themselves.

It's a question of respecting the basic atomic structure. In my Internet self-education ramblings, I've visited fascinating Web sites that illustrate the complex way that atoms are organized. Putting that concept together with the anthropologist Margaret Mead's ideas about the nuclear family, it becomes clear that people do not relate to more than one atomic family.

In other words, no one deals well with dozens of people. The maximum anyone is able to regularly interact with is a half dozen people. Groups of between six and ten people who know all about each other don't need outside control. Better to have six teams of six people each rather an unwieldy thirty-six member unit. All you have to do to make your life as a manager easy is to divide your employees in this organic fashion. Respecting nature makes for easy control systems.

At Semco, our units are always a size that permits people to know each other, understand the whole, and negate the need for excessive control. At any rate, we usually organize along the lines of a half dozen to ten people who directly interact.

Basketball teams, church groups, military units, and large families provide clear evidence that human interaction functions best on a small scale. Family members meet at Thanksgiving or when Grandma turns eighty, but they don't regularly deal with more than a half dozen relatives. Most don't even like a lot of their own relatives, which is why I always find it comical that business owners are looking for a company that is just one big family.

WE DO BUDGETS ON a small scale at Semco. Each group of six to ten people, once every six months, puts together the numbers for their unit. If they need help, they easily get it from the financial office. They organize their own work for the next quarter, and keep the vocal disagreements and heated arguments that sometimes fill the air within the cellular unit. When push comes to shove, the budgets have to come out positive. Nevertheless, whether they are biologists at ERM, engineers, or plant assembly mechanics in manufacturing, they know from the budget process exactly what's ahead in the coming months.

We believe that any company, even a Boeing, GM, or the U.S. Postal Service, should allow their workers to organize themselves, even when tens of thousands of employees are involved.

It could be done the same way we do it at Semco. It's not a question of size. Rather, it's a question of relinquishing control, trusting workers to pursue their own best interests, sitting back and letting nature take its course. This isn't an academic exercise for us. Self-management at Semco has been tested many times, often in tricky and unexpected ways that would be complicated no matter how big the company.

In 2001, we had a problem with theft at Semco headquarters. Someone was stealing personal belongings, things like purses, jackets, laptops, and cell phones. So many were stolen that it had to be an inside job. The thought that someone inside the company was preying on everyone else was both disconcerting and infuriating.

People became so upset they began clamoring for searches and security cameras. Clovis Bojikian, many other directors, and I resisted making any changes. I believe that measures designed to monitor people's activities are far more dangerous than any thief. We knew that eventually the workers were going to self-manage in this situation and decide for themselves how they wanted to deal with it. If they chose to install cameras, that decision would come in a company-wide referendum. I was convinced that cameras wouldn't solve the problem and would raise new debates about privacy issues, but I'm always willing to let the process play itself out because everyone learns best if they participate in real events.

In any case, the system at Semco does not allow me to impose my will on the company, even if I want to. Sure, I'm the main shareholder, so I always have a loaded gun in a drawer and the right to fire it, but understanding the benefits of our system is my self-restraint. I know that there's only one bullet in the gun, and if I fire it off in a fit of pique, I'll only get one shot at overriding a popular decision, after which I'll be disarmed. At that point, I'd lose everything I've worked for, and people would know that democracy at Semco was fleeting, insincere, and unreliable. That's too high a price to pay. Considering that I haven't pulled out my big gun in worse economic times, I wasn't about to use it over the hidden camera issue. In the end, the problem solved itself by simply fading away. The thievery stopped and the proponents of the cameras lost interest in the cause.

The most critical self-management crisis came in the early 1990s, when the Brazilian government enacted several emergency plans, including one that confiscated people's bank accounts, that wreaked havoc on our economy. We lost contracts in droves and couldn't meet payroll for two consecutive months. Banks failed and times were desperate. Our workers gathered at company meetings in the cafeteria. Many took turns at a microphone for long, emotional debates over the fate of Semco, and at the same time they wanted to understand the options for the company's future.

They'd already done everything they could think of to avert layoffs. They'd left their machines to sell spare parts on the road, severed contracts with maintenance, cleaning, and security providers to take on those jobs themselves. They'd driven company trucks in shifts and taken turns doing kitchen duty.

We'd long been practicing what we preach with open, shared information. We'd also been comanaging with the union, a system in which every check required a signature from management and one from the union. So Semco's numbers were well known to everyone, and workers and management trusted each other.

There was no denying economic reality in Brazil, however. The market was unyielding and sales were down too far. Whatever heroic measures the workers had undertaken couldn't be sustained indefinitely. More drastic measures were necessary and a decision had to be made. We'd have to close a factory and fire the people who worked there. The employee commission studied our numbers carefully and concluded that there was just enough money left in the till for a generous severance package.

The workers gathered in the cafeteria voted. They shut down the factory. Two hundred souls lost their jobs, and they elected to distribute the remaining cash between them.

Throughout this process, I opposed closing the plant. I

didn't want to empty the till in one stroke, and I was concerned about the emotional shock of padlocking a factory we had worked long and hard to build. I spoke against it and tried to persuade the workers to keep it open and to hang on for a few more months. When pressed, I had to confess that our cash cushion would only continue to shrink, so the risk that the workers would get no severance at all would increase. After much debate, they still chose to shutter the plant. Their pay at termination included our very generous terms of six to fourteen months' severance, nearly double the amount required by law. Many of those who voted to end their own jobs wanted to take their severance pay to start small businesses of their own; many started working for us as consultants and vendors. We even leased machinery from the closed factory to some who started machine shops, and we contract with some of them to this day.

I still feel pangs of sorrow when I think of those painful circumstances, but the workers were ultimately right. The Brazilian economy worsened, and had we extended our goodwill indefinitely, the workers would have been even more financially unstable in the end. They exercised their right to self-management in the most trying circumstances, when it meant eliminating their own jobs.

Self-management isn't limited to major decisions. It even applies to our security guards. We could have opted to train a particularly scrupulous guard who one afternoon turned away a Semco employee who came to work in shorts. The guard refused him entry, pointedly declaring that shorts were not acceptable. In fact, Semco has no such rule, but the worker returned home as instructed and changed his clothes. The story got around, and soon everyone was asking whether we had a dress code. We didn't reprimand the guard or clarify our dress code, or send the guard for additional training. Instead, we took no position on any of the issues and simply let debate take place. The matter ended when three guys from the ERM unit told the guards that there was no dress policy, and if there was one, they'd like to see it in writing. That ended that.

By giving up or sharing control of small, nettlesome issues like dress codes, and of graver matters like factory closings and security, management creates a culture of self-government that has more resilience than any my-way-or-the-highway dictatorship.

- ■ **Why is uniformity desirable?**

- ■ **Why do we practice age segregation?**

- ■ **Why not put the fox in charge of the hen house?**

EIGHT

SATURDAY

- Walk out of a boring meeting.
- Give the boss a lousy rating.
- Join the Board of Directors.

IF A SATURDAY BUSINESS meeting seems to violate the spirit of the seven-day weekend, don't let it bother you. A Saturday meeting is never a problem. If it is—don't show.

No one is required to attend any meeting at Semco. They're all voluntary. Everyone is invited, and people can come and go as they wish. If someone's self-interest is served by skipping a meeting or leaving early, it's perfectly fine. There is a constant ebb and flow at Semco meetings; people open the door and plunk down their things, gather papers and notebooks together, smile around the room, make their way elsewhere.

This kind of atmosphere leaves our international partners somewhat bewildered, and sometimes offended when one of us skips out of a meeting at what seems to be a critical moment. They're sometimes annoyed when someone waltzes in one hour after the meetings starts, listens for a while, makes a comment, goes outside to answer his cell phone, and never returns. The way we see it, if someone isn't interested in this particular project or meeting, we'd much rather have him conserve his energy for something else. We don't see a conflict if a Semco employee needs to spend an hour and a half talking on the phone to her teenage daughter instead of attending the powwow. If she doesn't feel a sense of balance between her personal and professional life, she's not going to do well at either one. While she may stay in the job because she needs the money, she'll quickly become one of those disillusioned people who does only what she must to earn her paycheck—and that's not the kind of employees we want at Semco.

If Semco forced workers to attend meetings, we'd never learn when projects or subjects are of no interest to the company's employees. If no one signs up to take part in a collective interview, then we've gained important information, namely that Semco employees didn't think the job we were trying to fill was important or necessary, so we'd eliminate it. The same thing applies to a new project that no one wants to work on. We say good-bye to it because that new service or product shouldn't exist until someone really wants to see it happen. Then it'll take off in no time. It's that simple.

I suppose it's a form of voting with our feet, and it extends to the self-managing operations. Everyone at the company is invited to participate in preparing the rolling six-month budget. Cynics say that it's impossible to put a budget together with input from dozens of people. Lucky for us we don't have dozens of people in every business unit who want to play with calculators and spreadsheets. Therefore, not so coincidentally, it's the financial types who always show up at budget meetings. The others are comfortable knowing they could have attended if they'd wanted, and that they'll nevertheless see the results, understand what happened, and still be able to question the outcome.

During these budget sessions, each unit plans how many people it will need for the upcoming six months, and they are included in the proposed payroll. There's quite a bit of open debate on these occasions, and it's not an easy time if business is poor. Often we end up with employees who are not on anyone's payroll. These people usually become nontraditional employees and reps, out-taskers, consultants, or part-timers.

It was during one of these sessions that we examined what really defines an employee. Marcio Batoni, CEO of the inventory business, unexpectedly asked whether our people should be formal employees at all.

Celso Violin, who has run our personnel office for twenty years, immediately replied that formal employees feel safer.

Warming up to his next why, Marcio retorted, "But why, if we can fire them at any time?"

"Because as formal employees they'll have a more stable

connection to the company," interjected Clovis Bojikian, the current guardian of Our Way of Doing Things. That prompted someone else to speak up.

"Why should they feel more secure as an employee than as one of the independent contractors who have been receiving paychecks from us every month for ten years?"

Once more, the debate was really about certain procedures that we take for granted. Once we asked ourselves why, we discovered many ways to create permanent relationships with workers without making them staff employees, but at the same time providing a stable ongoing partnership that fosters an independent entrepreneurial spirit without going overboard by imposing a sink or swim ethos. Does that mean stripping them of medical and retirement benefits, paid vacations, and the like? Absolutely not. These important features can be built into a vendor or consulting arrangement and made part of the fee structure. What's given a full-time worker can just as easily be taken away. Yet, an independent contractor gets to call her own shots.

For example, after Cecilia Balby suffered a miscarriage, she returned to work at ERM, but made it clear her priority was having a family. She didn't plan to work full-time, but she also wanted to buy an apartment. She decided to create her own company and sell her time to us as a consultant. Once she set herself up, she got even more responsibility and began managing a new area for Semco.

Soon Cecilia was pregnant again, and her doctors advised her to take it easy.

She came to the office only for the monthly meetings, and spent the rest of her time working at home. Other employees went to her place for meetings, which were held at the candy store on the corner near her building. The unit's sales goal was $300,000, and Cecilia reached half a million while working from home.

After much soul-searching, we concluded that a full-time employee only had to have one prerequisite, a material connection with the very heart of the business that makes us unique. We decided that the job had to be a central part of the difference between us and our competitors; the employee had to be more useful as a full-time, exclusive Semco worker, rather than as a part-timer who gains knowledge and vision by also working for other companies; and the connection between the company and the job had to be intrinsic and obvious.

This list generated much debate and more than a few screaming matches.

As usual, these ideas were not reached by consensus, or set out as policy, or carved in stone. When we don't have full agreement on something, we often leave the issue unsettled by accepting the fact that some people will follow the list while others ignore it. It's madness to believe that every issue requires a company policy. We don't go in for such rules and regulations.

Fully half of the people who wander our buildings and facilities are no longer traditional employees. This process has set many people free and opened entirely new horizons for others.

We've found that our litmus test for full-time workers—

that their jobs be central to what sets us apart from our competitors—doesn't always apply. Positions that should be staffed by full-timers are the ones that connect to our core businesses, jobs in areas such as specialized engineering and product application, geology and remediation experts, strategic thinkers, final assembly workers, or supervisors who oversee third parties in facilities management.

That narrows down the kinds of jobs that can be filled creatively. You'd be surprised who fits into that category. We do have directors in support areas who are no longer formal employees. They're all free to work for other companies, although many don't have the time or the desire to do so. They are also free to work for our competitors, and a few do. After all, if we cannot trust someone to be ethical and decide what information is confidential, we shouldn't be hiring them in the first place.

CREATIVE COMPENSATION

Over the years, our flexibility has even extended to pay scales. In all, we have eleven compensation options. They include fixed salaries, bonuses, profit sharing, commissions, royalties on sales, royalties on profits, commissions on gross margin, stock or stock options, IPO or sale. Under this last option, an executive cashes in when a business unit goes public or is sold. In addition,

A FLEXIBLE REWARD SYSTEM ENHANCES WORKPLACE DEMOCRACY AND WORKER SELF-MANAGEMENT.

executives set their own annual targets and the amount they are paid if they meet those goals.

Arguably, Semco's most controversial initiative is to let its employees set their own salaries. Pundits are quick to bring up their dim view of human nature, on the assumption that people will obviously set their salaries much higher than feasible. It's the same argument we hear about people setting their own work schedules in a seven-day weekend mode. The first thing that leaps to mind is that people will come as late or little as possible—and this has never been our experience.

The same applies to self-set salaries. What, after all, determines what an adequate salary is? To me, there are five items: three that the company knows, and two that the employee knows. And someone needs to have all five in hand to make the right decision.

The company knows what Hay or Price surveys tell them about what people make elsewhere, doing similar things. Second, the company knows what everyone inside it makes, and can make value judgments on a comparison basis. Third, the company knows whether its product, service, or current market conditions can afford above or below average salaries.

Employees, on the other hand, know two things that the company does not: first, what they'd intimately like to be making at this point in their career, based on how happy they are with their job and work/life balance and, second, what their spouses, neighbors, and former schoolmates are making.

By giving them the first three we finally have employees

who have all five criteria that make for a reasoned salary decision. We distribute copies of the market surveys so that they can know what people make at competitors, show them what everyone (from me all the way to the janitors) in the company makes, and openly present and discuss what the company's profits and prospects are.

In some fifteen years of this we can count on our fingers the people who chose to set their salaries at a higher level—and, of these, several were correct, and went on to make their desired numbers at other companies. Our loss.

At one point, about one-third of the company was on this system—we were slowly making our way through the wary middle managers and the inherent skepticism that comes with school-conditioned humanity. We even invented something called Monitored Self-Set Salary Process, whereby a manager would sign off, after a discussion with the employee, before determining the final number.

With rapid growth the conventional anchors of insecurity took hold again, and the one-third diminished. Now, we are again putting wood into the furnace, and the number of people that set their own salaries is climbing quickly again.

Semco's myriad of options can be combined in different ways. This flexible reward system mirrors our philosophy that people will understand that it's in their best interest to choose compensation packages that maximize both their own pay and the company's returns.

We offer these variations so that we have the flexibility to hire the people we need, even when times are hard, and we tie this to our practice of setting employment needs and goals during budget reviews. Employees themselves understand the link between a financially healthy and growing company and their own self-determined salary levels.

Anyone who requests too large a salary or too big a raise runs the risk of being rejected by their colleagues. So not too many people ask for excessive paychecks. We also encourage people to live within the budget limits of their own departments. That's why monthly revenue reports, budget reviews, profit-sharing plans, and transparent numbers are so important at Semco. If workers understand the big picture, they'll know how their salaries fit into it.

Many of our employees invest part of their salaries in profit-sharing plans, which earns them a greater return on their money than if they simply took the money home in a paycheck.

Francisco Alves Pereira, a mechanical assembly technician at Semco Processes, sometimes invests two-thirds of his raises in a variable plan. When his unit's earning goals are met, Francisco can take home the equivalent of three extra paychecks. On the other hand, if the unit fails to perform as expected, he could lose the entire sum of the raises, about 10 percent of his income. So Francisco takes an active role in how his unit performs. Like many employees, he knows his unit's numbers better than I do. Production costs are on the tip of his tongue, and he decides which equipment the factory will assemble.

My drive to Semco takes me past a cemetery, which is next door to my house and where my parents are buried. The sight often gets me thinking about my father, and when I enter the lobby of our building and pass a small bronze bust of him, I invariably greet him with a nod. As I climb the stairs, I measure how happy he'd be with Semco today. Sometimes I know he would be very satisfied; other times I'm not so sure.

It's a challenge to live up to the high expectations of a father who was a model of self-discipline, always stood ramrod straight, was always on time, and always carried out his week in precisely the same way. Without fail, he arrived at the downtown office at 8:15 A.M., returned home for dinner at 7:45 P.M., appeared at the golf club to tee off on Wednesdays at 6:50 A.M, and arrived at the Suvretta Hotel in Switzerland on December 27 every year.

This routine gave him a sense of security and solidity, which explained his bouncy step and his can-do attitude. Although repetitive, Dr. Semler was not a limited person. He'd be proud today, I think, although we didn't see eye to eye in terms of how a business should be run.

Compared to him, I am a Frisbee in the park, never knowing where I'm going to land next. Even if I've made appointments, I sit down after breakfast and list by hand the things I must get done that day. I cross out what I think can wait or be cancelled during the day or during the current week. At the same time, I often skip a scheduled meeting at Semco if I know that certain other people will be there, and my presence is not really vital. I rarely cancel appointments with outside third parties because I rarely set anything up.

Having answered e-mail while riding my exercise bike (e-bike) by eight, and having made my list of what needs to be done, I then have the day to look forward to, and that's when I practice my quirky type of leadership. First, I rarely do anything that someone else can do. I have a lot of faith in other people, as the employees at Semco will attest. I'm also not good on explanations or giving instructions. I might just send a terse e-mail to someone, asking them to find someone at a given company, and sell them a certain service, because it occurred to me the timing is right. Many times I'm wrong, of course, so people take my advice and e-mails with a grain of salt. But I'm also right a lot of the time. I see my role in the company as the guy whose job it is to constantly insist that we rethink everything. That's my most valuable contribution. As I said, I'm a catalyst, and catalysts don't have to keep exact office hours.

Lest you get the wrong idea, let me assure you that I work a hell of a lot! I'm wired into Semco issues nearly twenty-four hours a day, although I may spend only four to five hours with my butt in my office chair.

Otherwise, I often pick up my little boy from school and take him to a pond to feed the ducks or go out for a long and lazy lunch. Once a week or so, I take a nap midafternoon, lying next to little Felipe, who looks just like his grandfather and me, and I hug him while he watches a Bob-the-Builder video.

My mind, however, is always working in the background, like a software program that never stops. Bob's earth-moving machinery might inspire me to jot something down about a new product, or some less practical and more woolly idea that has occurred to me.

This may not seem like leadership in action, but it is. Successful leadership isn't dictatorship. It injects fundamental ideas and processes into the bloodstream of an organization and of individuals who see things the same way but lack the leverage to carry them out on their own. As a one-man or one-woman protectorate of a humane, sustainable business process, the leader sees to it that new ideas emerge and bloom when the timing is right. Dictators come and go, and when they go the dictatorship goes with them. When a true leader departs, the company he leaves behind is healthy, self-governing, vibrant, and intact.

Given our freewheeling style it may surprise you to know that at Semco our leaders and their methods are carefully assessed using a program called Seen from Below. Every six months, workers anonymously fill out a questionnaire that asks things like whether a boss treats his subordinates the same way he treats other managers. Thirty-six unchanging questions in all, workers answer each with a number from one to a hundred. We don't change the template, because we're only interested in relative ratings. A seventy score is good if that's the range a manager always receives, but that same score might be worrisome if the manager had previously always earned a ninety. Everyone sees their own scores as well as everyone else's. We've found the survey very useful since average scores have increased by two or three points a year for the last six years.

Managers are not obligated to act on their scores, but we believe it is in their own best interest to realize when subordinates are not happy. If they don't take action themselves to do their own jobs more effectively, they risk getting fired or moved.

At workshops outside Semco, participants tell me that they'd expect workers to choose leaders who are nice to them, even if those managers are ineffective. They also assume that employees favor bosses who are politically able but technically weak. But Semco's history proves that's not what happens. People will not follow someone they don't respect. Our employees know that their livelihood depends on the company doing well, and they won't support a nice but ineffective leader.

SOME THINGS ARE NONE OF MY BUSINESS

I was twenty-one when I took over from my father and became CEO. Shortly after I began work, an incident occurred that turned me into an instant petty tyrant. A trusted and highly valued manager was said to be having an affair with the telephone switchboard operator. I thought my employees expected action from me, so I puffed up my chest, took a deep breath, and fired the woman, who had been with us for many years. The manager, I decided, was much too valuable to let go. Thinking back on the incident now, it was a classic case of employer as paterfamilias—and father always knows best.

Years went by before I realized what a grossly unfair mistake I had made. It embarrasses me to think that the illogic of such a double standard persuaded me to act as I did. If the affair was immoral, why didn't I fire them both? Better yet, who was I to pass judgment in the first place? Since then I've heard many tales of affairs, drug use, and other so-called illicit behavior inside and outside the company. I take no positions on such matters. It's abundantly clear to me that our employees are responsible adults who make their own choices about their lives, and it's none of management's business.

If drug or alcohol abuse interferes with a person's work or disturbs the work environment of others, the employees themselves take action. In one instance, a group of employees regularly smoked marijuana during their lunch break away from the plant, then returned to work stoned. They still managed to do their jobs well, but nevertheless they were using drugs, and other employees insisted we take disciplinary measures. We finally demanded a stop to the practice when it became apparent that the employees high on marijuana could be seriously injured in machine operations.

I can hear the Consistency Police blowing their whistles. "Pull over, Ricardo, why it is that workplace safety justifies being a petty tyrant when it involves marijuana and not when it comes to workers who refuse to wear safety glasses on the factory floor?"

Got me there. Sounds like I was looking for a fig leaf to

cover my tyrannical nakedness when it came to the marijuana use, because on safety glasses I'm a strict believer in self-management. The safety glasses issue came up during a visit to Semco by the BBC when this book was being written. A member of the camera crew, who has photographed factories around the world, commented to me that he was surprised to see not a single warning sign about wearing safety glasses. Most factories are plastered with them.

I explained that when we hire a worker he or she is told simply that we think it's a wonderful thing that they have two eyes and that we hope they'll keep both of them. But we add that it is up to them to take the necessary precautions, and we will never mention the subject again.

The BBC journalist said he was amazed that he never found one Semco worker on the floor without glasses, whereas at factories sporting warning signs it was just the opposite—workers seemed to go out of the way to disobey and not wear the glasses. That observation gave me the opportunity to expound on the idea of treating workers like intelligent adults and, of course, to extol the virtues of self-management. And for those readers who have been conditioned by their lawyers to fear liability lawsuits, I would argue that if workers actually wore their protective glasses for a change, there would be no grounds to sue in the first place. As for the marijuana inconsistency, the best I can do is contend that stoned workers are not capable of behaving like intelligent adults. You may think that's a little lame. I'll pay the ticket issued by the Consistency Police and give it some more thought.

It's hard for a leader, especially a charismatic one, to avoid becoming synonymous with the company in the eyes of employees and the public. Equally harmful is that leader who believes all the hype and equates himself with the company. To avoid this trap, I believe a dedicated leader must physically distance himself from day-to-day company workings and continually decrease his influence.

I stepped back from Semco because I had evidence that anything else would strangle it. In the 1980s, when Semco was growing and I was well known, we rarely closed a deal without my presence. Everyone thought they had to talk to me. I wanted a company that could do without me if I got hit by a bus, shot during one of my trips through Afghanistan, or drowned in a felucca while slithering down the Nile. I like my trips—besides they're my opportunity to understand better how tribes work—and Semco had to be able to function without me.

I also want my customers to depend on the company, not on me. I learned this maxim from a client who owned a large chain of diners and bought his dishwashers from us at a heavy discount. He was a ferocious bargainer and often tried to go up the corporate ladder for even more rebates. When the unit general manager passed him on to me, I listened at length to his tale of loyalty and commitment. When he finished, I asked him the size of his current discount. I expressed utter shock at the size of his discount (shock akin to that felt by Claude Raines that there was gambling at Rick's place in the movie *Casablanca*), but immediately promised to honor it and also have a stern talk with the manager who'd authorized it. The customer hung up, relieved that he could keep the same deal, but knowing that deeper rebates were unlikely. After I'd done the same to a half dozen customers, they stopped calling me.

It's been twelve years now since I put my signature to anything—contracts, checks, or powers of attorney. At the same time, I've never approved any expenditure, capital project, or plan. I lobby for the things I believe in, I participate when I have something to add to the discussion, but most important, I try to remove obstacles and create new mechanisms that will reinforce the things that make Semco successful, namely worker freedom, democracy, and lack of control.

Stepping back from daily operations allows me to get involved in the newer businesses, and perhaps employees in those units get the impression that I'm important because I'm around. A perfect example of this took place when Danilo Saicali joined the Internet ventures unit and I went to a few meetings to smooth his transition period. I quickly stopped when I realized that everyone directed their questions at me. Instead, I let Danilo work his magic alone, and just eighteen months later, he became the acting president and CEO of the entire company.

IT'S IRONIC THAT I was credited with success or vision when in our first year and a half, all our new ventures lost money. Our people blamed the market, the economy, and everything else, except me. The fact was, some of the businesses failed because of my decisions, but my employees did not want to believe that The Man could be to blame.

I think Semco's great success can often be attributed to my absences. Nobody cancels meetings as much as I do. Nobody avoids projects as often as I do. I've been known to decide at the last minute that an important international conference call scheduled two months in advance is no longer necessary. I don't believe that conference calls go sour because I wasn't on the line or that deals go south when I'm not involved. Success doesn't come from one man alone; it stems from collective decisions that your colleagues and employees heartily support.

Anyone, at times, can fall into the irresponsible leadership trap. Celina Antunes, our director of facility management at Cushman & Wakefield Semco, is perpetually in a good mood. She's intelligent, thoughtful, and makes people feel like her best friend within fifteen minutes. Her lunch hour is spent with others every day, and there aren't enough lunches in the week to accommodate all the people who want to eat with her. Celina's charm, however, has created a tremendous problem. Every customer wants to know if Celina will be at the office or attending a meeting. I don't think we'll lose any customers if Celina is absent, but some of her colleagues believe we'll be at a disadvantage without her. Whether they realize it or not, they believe they don't need to work as hard or as creatively as long as Celina has the customer in the bag.

They learned I was right when Celina decided to take a year's sabbatical to study at Stanford. We missed her, but corporate life went

> **ARROGANT LEADERSHIP LEADS TO IRRESPONSIBLE LEADERSHIP.**

on. Not a single customer canceled because she wasn't around. A year later she returned, wiser for the year she spent away, and also in line for a better job at Cushman & Wakefield Semco, as COO, running all the unit's operations and marketing as well.

IT'S HUMAN NATURE TO look for a savior or a father figure in business. Our herd mentality prompts us to line up behind leaders like Lee Iaccoca, Jack Welch, or Lou Gerstner, but two things happen very quickly when a leader becomes a hero. First, employees begin to delegate upward, and second, the CEO starts to believe his own press, which invariably portrays him as a genius. He begins to view his employees as servants who are going to automatically execute his mission using his values, his vision, and his passion. He'll leave the executive suite for a weekend at a posh resort, put together a new business plan, come back to the office, and tell everyone what they're going to be doing. Aside from the fact that he could be wrong, there's another major problem: Even if the new plan doesn't mesh with their interests, talents, and skills, the workers will still do their jobs, but unenthusiastically. The result is a lethal combination— a possibly flawed business plan executed in a half-hearted manner. To avoid this, some executives hire consultants or do in-house polls. I've often heard top managers say they listen to the rank and file. Bravo! And then what? Having considered all sides, they side with themselves and do what they intended to do all along.

Under the circumstances, it's only a matter of time before the "genius" shoots himself in the foot; yet in many companies, it's difficult to remove a strong manager when his performance slips. Promotion tends to be a one-way street. The old rule—what goes up must come down—isn't necessarily true. Lateral transfers or demotion back to a lesser position are hard to pull off. Squeezing the trigger and firing a CEO becomes a last-resort option since replacing him will often rock the boat, and simple change becomes upheaval.

In theory, a board of directors should be able to handle a change in the top leadership without missing a beat. However, I've found over the years that many long-term leaders are too deeply connected to board members. Board members may have no relationship to a company other than sitting on its board. What they know about the operation they learn through senior management, and they quickly become beholden to a few people they know and trust. It's not surprising that CEOs relish this role of being the board's guide and mentor. From the standpoint of a bewildered board member, that may be the most comfortable way to deal with a situation when you don't know what you're talking about or voting on, but it rarely does a company any good.

It may explain why I've found that the time spent on any given item on a board's agenda is inversely proportional to its importance. People can only competently debate issues they understand intimately. For example, a capital allocation of $150 million is usually a one-hour item at a board meeting. Management doesn't want too many probing questions, and board members are reluctant to question such a large project. After all, thousands of man-hours have gone into preparing it, including much soul searching, careful planning, and expensive consulting. The project wouldn't come before the board if it wasn't important and worthwhile, right?

So deciding whether to invest $150 million doesn't take much time. For a marathon three-hour discussion, try parking space! That is something every board member understands intimately, cares about profoundly, and is willing to fight for. A debate about first-come, first-served parking, for example, will guarantee many hours of animated hollering. Once people see themselves walking in the rain to the building when a trainee has parked by the door, you have a hot item for the board's protracted consideration. The members can understand the implications—personally. And they can visualize them. In an ideal world, boards would only be permitted to act on issues that rose to this level of interest. A little parking space fervor directed at some truly important decisions—like downsizing, tax finagling, or moving production offshore—would go a long way.

I'VE YET TO REMEDY the occasional senselessness of our board's agendas, but at Semco we've created a good symbolic tool for preventing a compromising relationship from developing between the board and the CEO. For eight years, until 2002, we rotated the CEO job every six months, each March and September. At the moment, we're trying a fixed president and CEO, Danilo Saicali. In the future, we might try a new system, something totally different. Perhaps a secret CEO? Heck, I'm all for it if it would do the company any good.

Although we are presently taking a break from it, the rotation method has a lot in its favor since it renders the CEO a temporary figure, meaning his office is not responsible for the budget on a fiscal calendar. The acting CEO cannot be blamed or credited for the company's performance, and that makes the system independent of the CEO. Blame or credit falls on each manager and employee. The CEO should be the quarterback, not God. In a sense, it makes us like Switzerland, where many citizens have a hard time remembering their President's name. Solidarity comes as a consequence of collective action, and not from one personality.

TRIBAL ELDERS SITTING AROUND THE FIRE

We've also adopted a practical way to ensure that our board doesn't become isolated from the day-to-day operations of the company. Boards at some companies have made a name for themselves as a group of overdressed, overly serious, over elderly males (mostly) who meet in solemn and stuffy convocation with others of their own ilk in overly oak-paneled meeting rooms. They think of themselves in classic Roman terms as tribunes of the people; or more accurately, as tribunes of the shareholders. Aside from the fact that the tribunes were supplanted by dictators and that Rome was sacked by the barbarians, it's an outdated way to run a multifaceted company by putting the representatives of one facet in charge and excluding others. Sort of like setting up a democracy and only giving the right to vote to white male property owners.

At Semco, we've put together a mixed board, one that we feel understands the company and helps it make choices. We do stack the deck a bit. I hold one seat, and three are permanently filled with senior executives. Two rotate among senior managers, and two are held, on a first-come, first-served basis, by any workers in the company. Whoever signs up first gets to sit in on the next board meeting. It effectively means that a messenger and a secretary might leave their workplace saying, "Sorry, I'm late for my board meeting." We provide information about the agenda so that they can prepare to participate. We expect them to vote, and to cast ballots for the people they represent.

Everyone at the meeting has an equal voice, and nothing is confidential. Anyone in the company can request copies of the minutes. They can't take a copy, but they're free to examine them.

Semco's board has eight seats. For twenty years it gathered around an enormous table in a somber, impressive boardroom with dark walnut paneling. The table was removed when I was out of town. No one asked me first. They simply decided they needed the space for another purpose. I wasn't going to object anyway, since I was determined to move the meeting into our company garden and open the board gatherings even further. Bringing the board into the light was more than symbolic for us.

I don't always get my way. On the first day the board was to meet in the garden, I could tell trouble was brewing when I arrived.

Jose Violi, our CFO and acting president, and several others thought it was unrealistic to hold a board meeting in the garden.

They didn't quibble with my desire to undo the boardroom mentality, or to making the meeting open, but they thought having it in the garden was going too far. They felt silly. Further, they were armed with Power Point presentations, which require a darkened room. After a few minutes, all of us adjourned to a free meeting room.

Five or six of the faces were new to me, so I introduced myself. I explained that everyone in the room had a vote, and that anyone new to the proceedings was welcome to interrupt at any time. The newcomers included an administrative assistant from the inventory business unit, a purchasing agent from the machinery manufacturing area, a building manager from the facilities management unit, and someone from corporate accounting. Violi chaired the meeting, and opened with a pretty traditional agenda. The first item concerned future funding for Semco Ventures, which had invested in software and Internet businesses and lost over a million dollars in fourteen months. Several board members felt we should cut our losses. After a lot of debate, however, we voted to continue financing the unit, but to look for outside investors to take a stake in some of the companies. We wanted Semco Ventures to continue with its business plan, but the board simply didn't want to pay for it all. Representatives from the Ventures unit explained that they were actually doing well compared to the rest of the high-tech sector, but that did little to assuage misgivings.

The meeting continued with budget discussions on our rolling six-month forecast, cash flow projections, and the state of negotiations with our British partners in one of our environmental companies. We were fifty-fifty partners with the British firm, and they planned an IPO in London and wanted to buy some stock from us to be a clear owner. We tossed all sorts of ideas around, but the best one came from the young employee from facilities management. His creative solution was to tie half the buy option to a price/earnings multiplier, which was what the British wanted, and the other half to a minimum floor price, which made us feel secure.

Some might argue that this or any solution could easily have come from a staid, traditional board as well. That's surely true. The question is whether all traditional boards would guess that solutions could also come from a young employee attending his first board meeting. We don't advocate eliminating leadership, we just think that leaders should recognize their place and also their limitations.

When executives, consultants, and professors in the world at large agree that leadership is situational, in that different leaders arise in response to unique circumstances, and thus invalidates a fixed, all-purpose leadership model, mostly they are preaching a gospel they do not practice. Despite changing situations and circumstances, those same CEOs strive to remain in their jobs for years, the consultants hold on tightly to their client companies, and the professors seek tenure. The same is true in organizations. There are no methods for alternating power and leadership on a regular basis.

I once conducted a series of workshops for the Australian Management Institute. My favorite exercise was to invite half a dozen volunteers to the stage for a leadership skit. I asked them to pretend they were the few surviving passengers on a plane that had crashed in the Himalayas. I designated one as the captain, then asked the group to enact what they would do in the next twenty minutes. Within a few moments, a leader would emerge, and it was never the captain I'd appointed. Someone else would start dividing people into teams of two or three, one assigned to looking for water, the other to fixing the radio or signaling passing airplanes, the third to tending to the injured, and so on.

After a while, I would interrupt and ask them to consider another scenario. The same group would now be an activist environmental group that had heard that a large chemical plant was going to dump toxic waste into the river that afternoon. Almost immediately, someone would take over as leader, and it was never the same person who had led the plane crash survivors. In a few minutes, the new leader would suggest that one of them contact the press, that a second rally the workers, that a third get in touch with management, and still another organize a protest boat. On two occasions, the person I had chosen as airplane captain came through as environmental leader in this second exercise. These exercises reinforced my belief that leadership indeed depends on the situation. As circumstances change, leadership must change. A certain set of skills, instincts, and personality traits may be perfect today, but useless tomorrow.

The exercise also raises the question of whether leadership is necessary at all, or necessary in the context in which it is commonly defined and practiced. For better or worse, the modern organization is more like a plane crash or a chemical spill than it is the proverbial well-oiled machine. This is the era of crisis management, and that means doing business is all about administering first aid to the wounded and cleaning up the mess, not about orderly execution of a plan or policy. At some point in the process, self-management takes over. Self-interest and the survival instinct kick in. The group coheres as its components start to function according to their unique skills tempered by experience. From then on leadership, beyond acting as catalyst, directing traffic, and playing honest broker when conflicts arise, is superfluous. Moreover, in my view, obtrusive and intrusive leadership becomes counterproductive by interfering with the free interplay of individual talent and interest.

Situational leadership, as a concept, is reduced to farce when it is grafted onto top down, command-and-control leadership. It's ridiculous to assume that the boss, or a handful of bosses, know best how to cope with the chaos of a global marketplace, exploding technological change, and a wildly diverse workforce and customer-base—"situations" that common sense tells us need all the collective wisdom and talent that we can muster. Exchanging the old boss for a new boss is not situational leadership. True situational leadership—flexible, effective, evolutionary—can only arise from self-management. And that means that situational leadership doesn't change fundamentally with circumstances. It is always about giving up control.

BACK TO SCHOOL

Along with situational leadership, "flattening the organization" has gained favor as a catchphrase. I'm all for it—sort of. Hierarchies can become problematic when people feel they deserve to take control because of their title on the organizational chart. That's why we avoid the rights and perks that usually accompany the title, such as the corner office, the parking space, or the executive secretary. We're in favor of a hierarchy of self-interest and talent and opposed to the symbols of power and control that come with it.

Even so, these symbols still cause quite a fuss. Thirty percent of all issues in organizations are what I call boarding school stuff: rewards and punishments, how to dress, what time to show up, how to address superiors, how to behave properly. Even worse, they include fodder for the "green-eyed monster," jealousy, things like why somebody got a raise and somebody else didn't, why she got the better client account, or why he was asked to join the board.

One of my least favorite boarding school tantrums that occurs regularly concerns titles and business cards. At Semco, we tell people to put anything they want on their business cards. I myself don't use a business card, so I don't need a title. On the other hand, Joao Vendramim's card reads, Royal Pharoah in Charge of Supplies. Jose Alignani's card has his name on it, nothing else. Most people did the same, but when Ubirajar Freitas joined Semco, he decided on his own that he was a president. Soon customers and suppliers were tsk-tsking over what a shame it was that Jose Alignani, CEO at Cushman & Wakefield Semco, had been demoted.

This buzzing reached enough of a pitch that people inside Semco began urging Alignani to put president on his business card, too, but he refused. The issue came to a head when customers began calling Bira instead of Alignani because they wanted to talk to the president. Finally, I sent Alignani an e-mail suggesting that if his customers found it so important, he should print a card that says president, because the function of the card is to give the customers what they want. "If the customers need a president," I said, "we'll get them a president." So he finally agreed. Inside the company, Alignani's card means nothing, and that's true for everyone's titles and cards. At Semco, you are what you do, not what or whom you control.

- Why not make attending meetings optional?

- Why have a permanent CEO?

- Why are job titles important to the customer?

NINE

EVERY DAY

- Do some unexpected learning.
- Climb a decision-tree, but don't nest there.
- Sit back, relax, and plan only as far as the next bend in the river.

WHILE WRITING PARTS OF this book, I sat in the grounds of a fourteenth-century monastery in Sicily, watching two elderly gentlemen tend the ornate and precise gardens. Silence, of course, was the order of the day. Yet in the little nearby village I was always under the impression that a rabid family feud was in progress, but it was only Sicilians heatedly debating the relative merits of hanging clothes from the bedroom window or from the roof.

At the monastery I read books at night, one about the migratory navigation methods of geese, another about the patterns of brainwave flow that ensure motivation, and a third about Paideia, the Greek concept of an ideal education. When I read like this, I don't necessarily finish all the books; I'm indulging my endless curiosity and constantly shifting my position as onlooker in the world. It's akin to changing my seat in the auditorium of life when the stage is in the middle of a round theater. Sometimes I sit up front and see all the minute details, sometimes so far up and away that the stage is but a little box, and sometimes directly on the stage, wondering what I'm doing there.

WHEN I'M HOME, I like to sit with books in the garden or by a fire; or sit in front of a computer, navigating the Internet, and studying in a rambling fashion. Serendipity is my guide. My interests change from day to day. I may study the planets one afternoon, but a word I stumble across may lead me to Renaissance Italy or molecular theories.

Have I been thrown off my original road? Yes. But as Alice in Wonderland asked of the Cheshire Cat, "Which way should I go?" "It depends entirely on where you want to go," the feline replied. "Anywhere, as long as it takes me somewhere," said Alice. "In that case," the cat purred, "any of the roads will do."

In my life, anywhere I end up is somewhere I want to be.

For most people, this is fairy-tale talk, but I take it literally. Twice in my life I've gone to an airport, and only then chosen a destination. If I don't know where I'm going, any road is interesting.

After floating down the Nile from Sudan, riding a dogsled to the magnetic North Pole and retracing Marco Polo's route through Iran, Afghanistan, Kazakhstan, and Mongolia, I am now preparing for my fifth trip to Africa. Having gone from Zanzibar to Uganda, Congo to Madagascar, I'm now ready for two weeks of gorilla viewing in Rwanda and pigmy contact in Cameroon.

Each of these ramblings brings unexpected dividends, from throwing my watch from a camel's back fifteen years ago in mid-Saharan Chad, to viewing cloistered monks at a French Trappist monastery in the Atlas Mountains. In Rwanda, an insight into humankind might arise from contact with the Hutus, or from an emotional visit to the Nyamata genocide museum in Kigali.

Inside an organization, the road taken can also permit ambling, rambling, and unexpected learning. You just have to let go. As I've said, most business leaders find that difficult, if not painful, but ultimately profoundly rewarding.

For example, if I'm building an inventory-counting business by relying only on inventory specialists to guide me, there is no chance for me to accidentally stumble across, say, a new idea for a Web inventory clearinghouse. I'll never develop fourth generation supply chains, which Semco is doing now, or come up with a plan to bundle restocking, reordering, inventory management and loss prevention. Traveling the linear path, instead of allowing myself to roam, will limit my options. If I stay with what I know, I won't know what I don't know.

In our inventory business, we could have relied entirely on our partners' specialists, a sound approach, had we wanted to occupy that particular niche. If we'd like to split things up and explore ways to use the technology for other purposes, then we have to be open to utilizing people who understand the Internet or supply chains. They'll create different businesses for us. By the second or third incarnation, Semco's unit may become a company that our own partners don't recognize. Otherwise, the inventory business risks the same fate as the Boston trolley car business that once had a lock on city transportation. It becomes obsolete in the face of changing times, technology, and demand. That's scary to anyone responsible for planning, yet a lot of people prefer to stay in control and to control others, rather than stare straight into an unknown fraught with risk, potential mistakes, and unintended happy consequences.

REDUCING RISK

The desire to reduce the peril that comes with freedom in the workplace is understandable, but it carries its own burden of risk. A computer will never replace gut instinct, nor can numbers and financial discipline tell you unerringly where to go and what to do. Nevertheless, many people will assure you that if change is a constant, then computer-based strategic models offer solutions that are superior to so-called "emotional intelligence." What's more, this mainstay of conventional wisdom has been scientifically and laboriously tested.

In the early 1970s, a group of German professors in Munich decided to examine the conceptual validity of strategic execution supported by reams of data. They used an early Cray supercomputer to monitor an activity that had specific strategic goals and very limited variables—soccer. They spent over a year putting in all of the facts and figures available on the German soccer championship.

They studied player height, weight, and force of kick. They entered the strategy of the coaches, various athletic techniques, differences between the playing fields, the mass of fans, the effect of salaries, press coverage, and even wind speed.

They used the current and former tactics of each coach, the weight of the ball, player substitution, and even meteorological conditions to determine each team's strategy and its effect on the game. They conducted countless simulations. Then they followed one full season of the German soccer league.

After it was over, the researchers conceded failure. Not once were they able to predict a goal or a winning team. Yet in the same season, a punter at a traditional bookmaker in London had been right in eleven out of thirteen matches!

Chess is another example. Deep Blue, the supercomputer that IBM built specifically to beat the best human chess player in the world, was programmed to have access to every grandmaster game ever played. Early versions of the machine could ponder ten thousand chess positions a minute while phenoms like Gary Kasparov could consider three in the same amount of time. Still, Kasparov kept winning until 1996 when IBM engineers boosted the computer's capacity to consider the optimal move to 100 million positions a second! Even at that, Kasparov defeated the machine by winning three games to one loss (with two draws) to take the six-game match.

Kasparov had intellect, memory, agility, strategic vision, and complex mathematical capacity, but the machine always had more of those attributes. So there had to be another explanation for Kasparov's defeat of the silicon behemoth. To me, the world chess champion had only one thing that the machine did not—intuition.

And intuition is the fuel of choice for rambling through the seven-day weekend. The decision to turn left or right, stop or go, move fast or slow is guided by reason and experience. Intuition, however, is a form of knowledge that is independent of those explicit qualities, thereby imbuing action and perception with enlarged meaning. While all phenomena have obvious surface meaning or purpose, they also possess multiple layers of covert meaning and purpose. The intuitive are able to access those latter hidden dimensions. The term is maddening in its vagueness, and philosophers have gotten entangled in semantic webs of their own making. Nonetheless, the effects of intuition are real and will, I suspect, be pinpointed one day by research into the intricate workings of the human brain. The mystery of why some people are more in touch with their intuitive faculties has something to do, I believe, with the license allowed to the uninhibited use of those attributes. The grandmaster and bookie are paid handsomely to use their intuition and penalized for not acting on it.

A person who is told that she is not paid to think won't waste her time thinking, at least not about the boss's business, and her initiative will quickly dry up. Likewise, if she's admonished to do her job by the numbers or by the book, she won't cultivate her intuitive powers. She'll stick to the overt meaning of things and shun the covert. There will be no leaps of imagination or breakthrough insights. Her intuitive power will atrophy.

People have to be encouraged to act on instinct, because by-the-book managment leaves companies vulnerable, or otherwise its potency as a tool will be lost. In the summer of 2001, Semco was attacked by a computer virus that swarmed through our entire network. No one could stop it, and several of our IT managers could see that it was going to destroy the system in more than one unit. Still, they hesitated to shut down the main server for fear of causing worse damage or of crippling the entire company. The only person who took the initiative was a young woman who manages ERM's network. She thought that the best thing to do was to simply shut down everything until someone could stop the virus, and did just that without asking anyone's opinion or permission. In so doing, she was acting in accord with one of Semco's unofficial mottos: Better to beg for forgiveness than ask permission.

When the dust settled, it took two days to clean up Semco's main computers. The ERM system needed only a few hours of repairs. No forgiveness was necessary.

From our point of view, a computer virus is a serious disaster, but the failure to insist that workers act on their instincts caused a true catastrophe for one of our customers.

In 2001, engineers on a deep-sea oil drilling platform off the coast of Brazil discovered a bleed valve leak. They made a note of it in a memo and distributed eight copies to their supervisors, exactly as instructed in their manual. The leak caused an explosion, crippling one leg of the platform and eventually sinking the rig. It was officially labeled an accident, but in truth, poor communication made it possible.

Everyone knew the bleed valve leak was very dangerous. None were empowered to listen to his intuition, pick up the phone and call the president of the oil company and say, "This baby is going over!" None were conditioned to act on her own initiative. Fear of demerits, of discipline, or of losing their job prevented anyone from unilaterally deciding to turn off all the valves. Such a move would have cost two days production and millions of barrels of oil.

I can only imagine the conversation: "Why the hell did you shut down this platform for two days?"

"Because I thought it was going to go down."

"What do you mean you thought? Who told you to think? You were supposed to make a note and file the memo to eight people."

No one learns to think beyond the instructions in a manual if there's no room for intuition. But once people learn to rely on intuition and discover that it's welcome in the workplace, they can use it on behalf of the organization and to guide their personal ambitions as well.

It makes for a classic win-win, and it's no accident that I am hammering on this theme in a chapter titled Every Day. Only by making intuition an everyday commodity, can you gain the maximum advantage intuition has to offer.

FROM THE GUT

I once spent a few hours with the planning director of a major oil company who explained to me his intricate process for collecting data. With 110 people in his department and a bank of computers to support him, he produced five- and ten-year plans, along with twenty-year outlooks. Geopolitical criteria, geological surveys, outlooks for war, drilling, and transportation variables were entered into the system.

I asked him what his five-year plan of five years ago had predicted as the price of a barrel of Brent Crude oil for that month. His reply was $38.40, which was interesting since a barrel actually cost $18 at the time, less than half his forecast. That amounted to a slight $22 billion hole in his company's budget.

I then inquired whether intuition couldn't play a useful part in his calculations. "Ah, but I do use mine," he said. He kept a notebook to record his feelings about the future price of a barrel of oil. "What was your gut prediction for this month?" I wondered; $23, was the reply.

I wondered why he didn't rely on his intuition, bolstered by his experience in the oil industry. I suggested that it would certainly produce a more accurate outcome than the manipulation of a mountain of data.

I asked a blunt question: How did he keep his job when his official forecasts were so off the mark? "Ah," said the man with silver hair and thick eyeglasses, "I have the right to be wrong, but only so long as I am precisely wrong!" Talk about Alice in Wonderland–style logic!

Intuition is a fundamental tenet of how we conduct business at Semco. We not only welcome it, but look for ways to increase the frequency of its appearance around the office. One forum for intuition is our Go/No Go meeting. The purpose of the meeting is exactly what the name implies. We gather once a month to hear new ideas, and at the end of the session, everyone casts a "go" or a "no go" vote for potential ventures. The underlying idea is that if employees are free to pursue any project, they must be able to propose a concept and begin the process of turning it into a business. At Go/No Go, anyone with control over a budget, anyone who has an idea or is looking for a new project, and anyone who is just plain interested, can show up and participate. What this means is that some people who attend won't have the experience or background that might traditionally be required to make such decisions. We don't initiate studies or set up commissions. There's a discussion, and at the end of the meeting, a vote—go, or no go. When the people at Semco speak, it applies just as equally to me as owner as it does to any other employee. I have one vote, after all.

At one point, I had what I was sure was a brilliant idea to adapt the technology used in heavy-duty industrial dishwashers so that home models could wash everyday dishes in ninety seconds or less. I called a meeting to discuss this ingenious new business plan, and no one showed up. Not a single person at Semco shared my interest or enthusiasm for this new marvel in home technology. Even though I still thought it was a great idea, I had to shelve it. If I ordered people to work on the project, they'd do so only under duress, perhaps ensuring that it wouldn't succeed.

Some months later, a competitor produced a similar machine and presented it with a blast of fanfare at a trade show. "You see, you see!" I would think, as I prowled our corridors with their new brochures, ready to hand them out to anyone who hadn't shown up at my meeting.

A year and a half later that competitor gave up on the dishwasher, and I quickly threw away the brochures. As I walked the halls of Semco, I could tell it was killing people not to shout: "You see, you see?!" as I passed by.

The fact is that only the very arrogant and the very naïve imagine that decisions have to be made at the

> ONE CANNOT IMAGINE THAT EVERY "BRIGHT" IDEA HAS MERIT JUST BECAUSE IT CAME FROM THE OWNER OR FROM SOMEONE ELSE AT THE TOP.

top, or close to Numero Uno. Power and position do not guarantee infallibility or even necessarily the best thinking. Democracy, of course, entitles people to disagree; the intuition of the majority overrides the power of the one. When voters reject a candidate or a proposition, they could be making a terrible mistake. But we regard their collective judgment and intuition as preferable to one man rule. Yet one man rule is somehow acceptable in a business context? I don't get it. You could argue that Thomas Edison's assistants would have killed many of his inventions, and GE along with it, but who knows how many bad ideas were indeed quietly aborted by assistants ("You see, Tom, you see?"); how much of that energy was refocused on something feasible; or how much collective support was needed for his inventions to finally succeed.

So it should be in business today. In a system where collective effort produces successful products, the only way to get your ideas off the ground is to lobby ferociously in favor of it. If no one buys into it, then leave it on the back burner and return to it later. In the end, if no one takes a passionate liking to it, the idea will simply die. And that's probably for the best.

IN PRAISE OF KOOKS

Sometimes, when I'm adamant and think that no one is seeing the merits of a new idea, I call in the kooks. I love kooks. Anyone who visits my garden at home knows this. The woman who planned and executed it, a seventy-year-old landscape architect of Russian origin, had asked for ninety days and one assistant to create it. I gladly accepted, even though I had heard that she was quirky, unstable, and suffered from manic depression. Twenty-six months and twenty-nine workers later, the garden was ready. As a CEO, I would have been fired eight times in the two years she worked on that garden, but it is now a model for landscapers as well as an endless source of pleasure, with its two-hundred-million-year-old boulders, underground waterways, and three-hundred-year-old elephant paw trees.

The same is true for the intricate music room that I built in the back of that garden. It took a group of specialists from Oregon and a zany acoustic expert in Brazil a full seventeen months to tune the room with blue and pink noise generators and create a Mecca for audiophiles.

Sometimes, to execute cutting-edge ideas, you must welcome unorthodox people and the workings of their eccentric minds. Peter Kuhlmann of RGIS remembered sitting in my sound room: "You went to great length to explain the system as well as its unique components. Then you had each of us sit in what you called the 'sweet spot.' I was thrilled when it was my turn and you were about to put on some music. I envisioned some Mozart or Liszt, maybe some Beatles, or, would I get lucky enough to hear Elvis? Nooooo! You played a friggin' garage door opening and closing. This I will never forget." Peter is too polite to call me a kook, but perhaps I am.

The danger of hanging out with kooks to bring wild and

crazy dreams to life is that you may lose contact with reality. But then it takes some of each extreme to create the extraordinary. So although I've ceased playing garage doors for people (a well-known test for audiophiles, I will add in my own defense), I still look for slightly crazy people to mix with our sane ones. It guarantees that intuition can come to the fore, and supplant the safe, familiar path. Excellence depends on following intuition to strange places.

Intuition is responsible for two Semco businesses that I wouldn't have invested in, but for the insistence of two of my colleagues. Jose Carlos Reis de Magalhaes, or Zeca, has always believed in the need for cell-tower management, and I found it interesting, which is another way of saying that I wasn't for it or against it. Initially, however, as we went through the business plan at a Go/No Go meeting, several grandiose assumptions struck me as too optimistic, and I lost faith in the project. But the business plan was approved without me, and the unit exists. It still hasn't proven itself, but we continue to invest in it because the majority of my staff has a gut feeling, or intuition, that this venture will succeed.

Another good example of profitable instinct at work is Semco Econsult. Eugenio Singer, the CEO of Semco ERM, wanted to buy Econsult in 1998. Established by four environmental engineers, it specialized in solving air pollution problems and establishing health and safety standards, but its numbers were poor. It had only twenty employees and did no more than $300,000 of business per year. I couldn't see much merit in it.

There was no material evidence that this would be a good fit with us. It would cost Semco $150,000 and could drain away a significant amount of management's time. In other words, we could be dedicating management horsepower to something that was never going to be very big. To his credit, Eugenio insisted, declaring in his business plan that he could turn Econsult into a $1 million a year business in five years. We all shrugged our shoulders.

In 2001, ERM Econsult held a conference in Bahia for ERM people from all over the world. It was the most profitable unit at Semco ERM, and one of the most profitable in the ERM Group worldwide. Eugenio's hunches played out.

MONEY DOESN'T GROW ON DECISION TREES

To the dismay of accountants and executives, I've often said that business plans and budgets are nothing more than extrapolations of wishful thinking. I frequently offer, only half jokingly to spend twenty minutes putting together a five-year plan for any company. If I have their numbers from the past two years, all I have to do is make the revenue and profit projections rise 5 to 10 percent per year. If this seems simplistic or silly, just look around for a company that forecasts it will grow 7 percent, then drop 4 percent, then merge with a competitor, then rise 8 percent, and then fall another 11 percent. I've never seen a business forecast like that, even though that's how most end up. They all show their numbers getting bigger every year, rendering the exercise useless.

Decision trees, a tool commonly used by financial analysts, are usually very confusing because, as my physics teacher helped me to understand, you can go only halfway into a forest of decision trees. After that, you're on your way out, and will have no idea you're exiting until you've reached the other side.

Information supports intuition, and that's why we make our facts and figures available to everyone, from assembly line workers to senior executives. Businesses usually want such information to project numbers into the future, but precise facts and numbers are only helpful if they're used to enhance decision-making, not as the basis for it.

I think even less of extrapolating numbers to predict the future. Projecting numbers into the future can explain business mistakes, and it also explains why economists are frequently off the mark, and why serious scientists who forecast population explosions, food shortages, and environmental disasters have often been so wrong.

At Semco, we use available data scrupulously to avoid gossip, rumor, and guesses. In general, businesses tend to be very insular and, even after decades, I'm continually shocked by the fact that most companies don't know much about their own industry or their competitors. They don't understand their own partners and suppliers, the size of their market, and what the competition might do next. Wild guesses are more common than solid information, and they are often repeated until they become the gospel truth in an industry and the source of imitation among rival organizations. We always strive to avoid that trap by using our intuition instead of guessing.

The dot-com frenzy is an example of the folly of using guesswork instead of intuition. The business plans presented in that high-tech gold rush were appallingly primitive. They were all predicated on an "if this, then that" formula to project potential demand for a business idea, and included a wide range of dangerous assumptions, many based on greed and ignorance, not informed intuition. Decisions are guided by reason and experience, with intuition serving as another form of knowledge that enlarges meaning. In other words, intuition hinges on reason and experience. I examined at least a hundred Internet-related business plans, and we put together about twenty of our own. All of them, including ours, were unhinged—totally divorced from reason and experience. We made the same silly assumptions about the industry, and I told investment bankers that I believed it was all pie-in-the-sky, but it didn't seem to matter to them.

The dot-com industry was based on plainly stupid premises, and the venture capitalists couldn't have missed it any more than me. But there were enough early successes that lined the pockets of people looking for an enormous short-term upside that it brought in even more investors. The money was there, it was ready to move, and all the investors needed were a few well-dressed business plans to ferry it, because the assumption was that all past knowledge was suspended. No, if we had really listened to our intuition instead of our greed and ego, we would have asked where does reason come down on this? ("Forget about it!") What does experience show us? ("Are you crazy!") And the dot-com bust wouldn't have done such horrendous damage.

From our painful dot-com lessons, we've learned to rely only on available data. Semco employs an editor to create a daily digest of major business news that is e-mailed to everyone. It focuses on issues and developments that might affect the company or one of its business units; it's easy and quick to read, essentially a headline with a link to a more detailed story.

We track our competitors' hiring practices by scouring newspapers, trade journals, and the Internet. We track many of their Web home pages, and we've learned to read between the lines on those sites. In each of our business units, one or two employees collect business information on a rotating basis.

Frequently, it is the obscure tidbits that have a serious impact on an industry or business. The information that really affects an organization is rarely part of a cataclysmic event. Rather, it is buried in small developments, like a slight change in direction that will not be detected in the immediate future. We don't summarize or reach conclusions, we just put the information out for employees to peruse. We also subscribe to a service that contains evaluations of our competitors' companies by investment bankers. We probably supply our people with more intelligence than the average company, but it's hard to track how they use it. We hope it's nothing more than fodder for intuitive thinking. When we add our own firsthand observations or conversations to the picture, the information becomes three-dimensional. Our people are thus better informed, more conversant in issues important to them, and more confident about their knowledge. That allows them to do what we want them to do—to follow their gut instincts.

At times, intuition can lead to mistakes, although maybe less often than numbers-based decision-making. We've made our share of intuitive mistakes at Semco. Life is full of mistakes. But you won't catch me subscribing to the new age management mantra—to err is human, but erring twice is not so hot. I don't buy the notion that we must carefully study our mistakes in order not to repeat them.

There was a marine engineer who, when I started at Semco, designed the pumps and motors that we sold to the shipping industry. He was a wise and experienced manager named Rubin Agater, and many customers would order pumping systems for two or three identical ships at a time. Rubin would always remark that there are no two things as different as two identical ships.

The same thing is true about mistakes. Nothing is as difficult as transmitting experience from one person to another, or from one situation to another. My father wanted me to take over Semco while he was still alive so he could help me learn to run the company. His chief concern was to catch my mistakes before I made them. I made a long series of mistakes that my father never saw coming because they were made in different circumstances than those he knew so well.

It's a fallacy that mistakes only

> **NO TWO THINGS ARE AS DIFFERENT AS TWO OF THE SAME MISTAKES.**

teach us what not to do. A perfect example is the tarte tatin considered as a business case. This famous French apple tart is the result of a mistake. One day, the two Tatin sisters who operated a little train station bistro in the village of Lamotte Beuvron were running late and didn't make enough pastry for their standard apple tart. To save time, they whipped up a batch of pastry, threw it on top of the apples, baked it just fifteen minutes, and turned the pie upside down when they took it out. Voila! Tarte tatin! And the mistake keeps happening millions of apples later.

We know that countless important discoveries resulted from mistakes or from serendipity. People were looking for one thing and tripped over another—including Columbus mistaking the West Indies for Asia and the discovery of penicillin when scientist Alexander Fleming who, instead of discarding a lab sample accidentally contaminated by mold, noticed that the mold was devouring bacteria. Luck is a most necessary component of success. But to accuse people of being lucky is usually unfair. Luck stems from effort and crowns a compulsion to succeed. Readiness is all. When luck strikes, you need to act with diligence to get the outcome you desire. Winning the lottery isn't luck, it's an accident. Spending the proceeds wisely is luck.

Intuition, luck, mistakes, serendipity—there you have four vital business concepts that every manager should know. Most organizations, however, wall themselves off from the four behind a barrier that's erected to ensure control. I say: Lighten up. Breathe. Let intuition, luck, mistakes, and serendipity happen. If Columbus, Aristotle, Newton, Fleming, et al are any indication, it may be the real formula that we need to go from good to great.

In my case, using my nose instead of a spreadsheet means that people are always asking me whether it makes me nervous to have no idea what the company will amount to in another five years. The truth is, it doesn't make me nervous at all. Abraham Lincoln said it best when asked how he planned to guide the United States after the Civil War: It's like piloting a riverboat on the Mississippi. You should sit back, relax, and plan only as far ahead as the next bend in the river, and then the one after that, and the one after that. Eventually, you'll get to your destination. He was right, as was Lewis Carroll's Cheshire Cat who said that "any of the roads will do." Although the cat's advice may be maddening to those who want to leave a boardroom with the certainty they know where they are going, it is sound technical strategy nevertheless. The cat wants us to accept the fact that we're not masters of our own destiny and that his advice won't spare us from having contentious meetings to brainstorm ideas or to endlessly juggle budget figures. The cat's kind of rambling is not a cavalier, who-cares approach. In fact it demonstrates a keen understanding of human nature where the reason and experience that go into sophisticated plans hinge on intuitive hunches, luck, mistakes, and serendipity.

By saying "any of the roads will do," do I sound like I'm preaching passivity? On the contrary, it's a bold doctrine, indeed. By recognizing that we possess the talent to make a success out of the most unlikely circumstances, we are freeing ourselves to go anywhere, do anything, and achieve great things. True passivity is taking the easy way out by trying to control the variables. But uncontrolled variables are what make dreams come true. If we change the way work works we can live the dream of work-life balance and sustainability.

A SAFETY MECHANISM

Change is often used by business as a scarecrow or a lucky rabbit's foot to ward off evil. As an IBM CEO once put it, "We only restructure for a good reason, and if we haven't restructured in a while, that's a good reason." A fine turn of phrase, but questionable logic. I smell fear. He was really saying that we are scared that competitors, technology, and consumers will put us out of business, and so we change all the time in order to stay alive. It's a variation of the old maxim, "a rolling stone gathers no moss." A changing company—a rolling company—can outrun the sins of its own past mediocrity. Got a problem? Change. Still got a problem? Change again. Change has become the all-purpose solution.

Yet change adds fuel to the bonfire of anxiety. It accentuates the desire for stability, and drives an organization toward traditional patterns of behavior—i. e., command and control—that creates a paralyzing culture clash. Change cannot coexist with the status quo unless it is trivialized or directed at a secondary target. That's why structural change starting from the bottom is popular. Top down change rarely occurs because the management tribe typically prefers to lay the burden on the employees rather than hoist it onto its own shoulders.

No wonder "change, change, change" has become a management chant. I think that change—defined as the act and fact of becoming fundamentally different— is vastly exaggerated, and a good example of that is the automobile. In the last one hundred years, the auto industry has spent tens of billions of dollars on research and product development. Henry Ford's first car had a metal chassis with an internal combustion, gasoline-powered engine, four wheels with rubber tires, a clutch assembly and brake system, a steering wheel and four seats, and it could safely do eighteen miles per hour.

A hundred years and tens of thousands of research hours later, we drive cars with a metal chassis, an internal combustion, gasoline-powered engine, four wheels with rubber tires, a clutch assembly and brake system, a steering wheel and four seats, and the average speed in London in 2001 was seventeen-point-five miles per hour!

That's not a hell of a lot of return for the money. Ford evidently doesn't have much to teach us about change. The fact that they're still manufacturing cars is not proof that Ford Motor Company is a sound organization, just proof that it takes very large companies to make cars in great quantities.

Fifty years after the development of the jet engine, planes are also little changed. They've grown bigger, wider, and can carry more people, but those are incremental, largely cosmetic changes.

Taken together, this lack of real change has come to mean that in the travel industry, whether driving or flying, time and technology have not combined to make things much better. Safety and design have improved, of course, but the basic assumptions about the final product remain the same.

The same is true for telephones, which relied on land lines instead of cellular technology for more than a hundred years, or the basic system of photography, which only recently has undergone a digital revolution.

The trivialization, perhaps a better word is marginalization, of technological change leaves business organizations prey to sabotage from within. When management heaps change on employees, and it's not in their self-interest, they withdraw their most valuable assets—passion, talent, and commitment. Crippled, business resorts to "defense by emulation." What I mean is organizations both large and small adopt common structural and behavioral patterns that extend industrywide, economywide, and worldwide. The prevailing business model ends up being based on the likes of Ford, Boeing, or Verizon, the bulked up, muscle-bound enforcers of corporate control. This industrywide emulation is poison.

In the 1960s, German auto companies developed plans to scrap the entire combustion engine for an electrical design. (The same existed in the 1970s in Japan, and in the 1980s in France.) So for forty years we might have been free of the wasteful and ludicrous dependence on fossil fuels. Why didn't it go anywhere? Because auto executives understood pistons and carburetors, and would be loathe to cannibalize their expertise, along with most of their factories.

Entrenched practices lead to industrywide emulation. Think about it—even though auto design changes every few years, the alterations are marginal. And everything that happens converges with industry trends. Line up eight midsized sedans at a distance of one hundred feet, and you won't be able to tell which company manufactured which vehicle. Place a Honda, a Ford, a GM, a Renault, and a Peugeot in a row, and you will find it impossible to distinguish among them unless you happen to own one.

Why? Because their designers all learned from the same books, went to the same schools, meet at the same conventions, attend trade shows together, and focus unduly on their competition.

Take the example of parallel parking. You must slide alongside and just beyond an empty spot, and then drive diagonally backward. I've been doing this for twenty-five years and am still unsure how it will turn out. Is there a sillier exercise than parallel parking? Yet it remains unchanged for the last one hundred years. Why? Because the engineers who design cars understand the basics of the automobile: It goes forward and backward, but it doesn't move sideways. Is it so difficult—with billions of dollars available for research—to create a simple mechanism that pivots the front and back wheels at an angle to the car so it can move sideways? Wouldn't I then simply approach a parking spot and instead of backing up, press the swivel button to rotate the tires, and glide sideways toward the curb?

Is it easier to put a person on the moon than to update parallel parking technology?

Think also about the music industry. Some of the giants around the world have devoted tremendous resources to creating music disks with secure packaging so people can't steal digital recordings from store shelves. While CD manufacturers focused on producing theft-proof boxes, along came an upstart called Napster and a technology known as MP3.

How many people have unopened CDs languishing on a shelf in their original packaging? Whoever invented the shrink-wrap and stickers that protect the disk should be working in Fort Knox by now. Shoplifters, of course, know how to quickly slit open the package and remove the CD. But simple, lower life forms (the customer) must use teeth, pens, razors, paper clips, and special openers to get at the CD. The kids at Napster made this feat of safety engineering a milestone in stupidity. And unraveled the music industry while they were at it. But the CDs are still safe in their plastic fortresses.

Examples abound. Take the airline industry. Not only have the executives who run the airlines made flying one of the most painful experiences in history, they've also failed to make sustainable money out of it.

Think, also, of the safety instructions on board each plane. Ever since I was six years old and flew Air France 707s from Dakar to Paris, I've been listening to instructions on how to use the flotation device under my seat. I'm sure I have heard some five hundred such presentations. I am equally sure that I would never know which strings to pull when an emergency arose, and would not, for the life of me, know where to blow, and whether to put mine on first, or my child's.

So why not join two of the most boring circumstances in modern life? One is safety instruction on board a plane. The other, sitting around in airports for much longer than necessary, because airlines want you there well before they're ready for you.

Couldn't the airlines arrange to have safety certificates given out in the waiting lounges? All you would have to do is present yourself, and someone would give you a ten-minute course (and you could put the life vest and oxygen mask on yourself). Maybe you'd even have to take a little test—the engineers would love that. Once tested, you'd be issued a certificate that was valid for, say, five years. And you'd show that every time you checked in. The crew would thereafter be absolved from the ridicule of waving their arms to passengers who politely ignore them, and the passengers would be saved the irritating repetition.

Or take the outrageous example of Gillette and the razor blade.

King Gillette developed the single razor at the beginning of the century. He had dreams of making a fortune when a friend suggested that he concentrate on a product—any product—that was disposable. Thus the razor. From this early triumph, Gillette thrived for decades. It was a fabuously successful company—one of the few that Warrent Buffett pegged as a solid gamble. Then Gillette concluded that the product required an overhaul, and spent millions on the TracII—basically the same product with an extra blade. But Gillette's executives couldn't leave well enough alone. In the 1990s, they took another unbelievable step: They spent $600 million to develop a completely new razor system. After this vast expenditure (complete with endless meetings, brainstorming sessions, and multiple-committee work), they unveiled their new invention: the Mach 3—a blade inserted between the other two!

I've often pointed out in my workshops about corporate architecture and control—that anyone in the room could have come up with the same idea if given a couple days to think about it. The price tag would certainly have been a lot less.

Change works well only if it is a nonissue. An organization that constantly, and artificially, coaches its people to change (accept change! recognize change!) is like a Darwinist standing next to a giraffe, shouting: "Stretch that neck! Stretch that neck!"

So how do we suddenly tell people to love risk? To toss aside everything they know about pistons and carburetors, for example, and make a headlong leap into electric cars?

By replacing control with democracy, by allowing employees to choose their own managers, and think and act independently. The first step toward creativity and confidence must include internal movement. Move people around from job to job, department to department, unit to unit. Mix and match. This blocks the human tendency to concoct feudal systems and erect fortresses. Those may guarantee security within the group, and protect against the change and risk that might emerge from the outside. But insecurity and change are what we are after at Semco.

Change also means that a company must be willing to shed or undo elements of itself that no longer have a future. It must be ready to unilaterally sell, spin off, or close units—it must be ready to cannibalize itself.

This continues to raise problems even at Semco. Many times when we have elected to cannibalize ourselves, the protective spirit of our employees surges, they close ranks around the relationships they have with one another, and they take the ostrich's approach—let's protect ourselves at all costs. They shy away from a new technology if adopting it will destroy their accustomed base.

But then we run another risk—the one that arises when you're too comfortable with what you're doing.

That's why we are dismantling our headquarters, and selling or loaning our industrial machinery to former employees who are now subcontractors. Keeping either makes no sense as a long-term plan. At the same time, workers inspired by their own cottage industry will take better care of the machinery, the computers, the hardware than if they just passed them every day on our factory floor. If they are producing and delivering parts to us from their own garage shop, they'll understand efficiency and profitability, rather than worry about the factory, the sixty other lathes, and the seventy people they labor with side-by-side and whose children they've watched grow.

They may not be able to bring themselves to cannibalize in that case. But in all likelihood, someone else will. And the process of change will continue regardless of all the kind hearts and coronets.

CONCLUSION

"What you are essentially advocating at Semco is harnessing the wisdom of people," a friend once told me. "Their reservoir of talent, the natural wisdom of the system, the wisdom that only comes from freedom, the wisdom that emerges however unevenly from democracy. Wisdom is what you get by asking why. . . ." I wish I had said that first, but I didn't so I'll second it. Essentially our company believes that we can take that wisdom to the bank this year, next year, and for decades to come. Semco's most precious asset is the wisdom of its workforce, and our success grows out of our employees' success.

And that's very good news, indeed. Although globalization was supposed to create a global village, one of free trade, technology, and open communication, much of the world still suffers the consequences of acute structural crisis. The term free-market capitalism is more of an oxymoron than ever. An era notable for the fall of the Berlin Wall has seen the systemic walls that surround the workplace remain intact and, in many ways, loom higher.

Lenin's and Stalin's form of communism is gone, yet its trappings have been expropriated by mega-corporations. We have companies featuring central planning by troikas, mission statements crafted by apparatchiks, five-year plans, no right to choose leaders in companies, no democracy in the workplace, a clear distinction between intelligentsia and peasants (top CEOs make 152 times the median salary and enjoy company dachas, jets, and limos), and state monitoring (time clocks, dress codes, drug screening, "employee assistance" plans, e-mail monitoring, no smoking, and other personal conduct rules, as well as family-life audits). Technology hasn't freed more time for leisure. On the contrary, it has eaten away at the weekend and left it devoid of the power to restore strength and happiness to the souls of those who toil.

Global companies don't practice democracy. You might argue that the shareholding structure is democratic, that each share contains the right to vote in an annual assembly of investors. But that's not democracy, and you can tell by sitting at a shareholder's meeting—just look at management's grip over companies, the board's lack of small shareholder representation, and the dictatorship of stronger investors over weaker ones. Add to that all the family businesses and companies that have one majority partner each, and you've got an overwhelming number of organizations that dispense with democracy as an unnecessary and senseless constraint. In its place, a structural hybrid has taken root that mutated out of the crossed genes of war and of twentieth-century totalitarianism.

Global capitalism today fits Winston Churchill's view on democracy: It's the worst system, except for all the others. But that's hardly reassuring.

As a consequence, the number of poor people in the world is increasing steadily, despite constant increases in GNP and lip service about the benefits of globalization and shared wealth.

I believe the time for organizations designed on the twentieth-century model is over, especially those based unknowingly on the Communist or military models. Redesigning the sustainable workplace for the twenty-first century means letting in fresh air and giving up control. That's easy to say, and hugely difficult to do. Asking why is terribly distracting for most CEOs. Managers aren't looking for ten- or twenty-year change programs—they want simple, objective goals: profit, growth, healthy quarterly reports, trained people, orderly markets, competitive advantage. Until these organizations face reality, give up the futile quest for control and begin to respect such concepts as workplace democracy, the need to question everything, and the search for a more balanced existence, even the most modest goals will be beyond reach.

Semco's case history and its consistent performance ($100,000 invested in Semco twenty years ago would now be worth $5.4 million) vouches for our financial success. If this book has planted the smallest seeds of doubt in anyone inclined to be wedded to the past, and more substantial kernels of hope in those actively looking for a better way, writing it will have been worthwhile.

Readers who are not managers may be intrigued with what they find here, but I fear that many will be frustrated because they won't believe it applies to them. Adopting the Semco way seems out of reach; they have no power.

But they are wrong. We all have enormous amounts of latitude, be it with our children, in social gatherings, or at work. Ideas underpinned by values are living things and forces to be reckoned with. Let's apply them to the workplace too. Let's understand and reject the temptation to bow to the command-and-control legacy. People who trade rush hour for idleness or who think about what they are doing in a new light—in other words, people who start living a seven-day weekend— can make a dramatic difference for themselves as well as for others. People who have two employees working for them can change two, five, or ten lives. That's a lot of significant, sustainable change.

I remember reading about a company where employees came up with practical solutions to a difficult situation. The director exclaimed: "Ah, I can see you've come up with a plan that works in practice. . . . But will it work in theory?" Good question, and since this book has been my attempt to reconcile practice and theory and make it useful to you, I'll share one final story.

A perfect convergence of practice and theory occurred a few years ago when I was once again rambling around the streets of midtown Manhattan, on my way to a meeting at the Citicorp Center.

Unlike my casual, spur-of-the-moment Cushman & Wakefield expedition, this time I was the very model of a modern major deal-maker in hot pursuit of an acquisition, the divine predatory right of those who find themselves swimming near the top of the food chain. My minnow du jour was the Reliance Corporation, a division of Exxon. I was well prepared, well financed, and well dressed.

I arrived precisely at five in the afternoon when the occupants of that silvery, fifty-nine story skyscraper all suddenly realized they were free to go home, or to at least get out of there and spend what was left of their day someplace else, doing something else with someone else. At first, I would have described it as a stampede, but there was nothing irrational, blind, or panicky about it. Quite the contrary, thousands of people were on the move, fast, and in the same direction—straight out the door.

Wave after wave of Nike, Adidas, and New Balance. Sandals, wing-tips, and boat shoes. Flats, heels, and clogs. All producing an ominous, low rumble of sound that stopped me in my tracks.

There was no way I was going to fight my way though that. I stepped back a safe distance and watched the revolving doors whipping around wildly, like the blades of a threshing machine furiously chewing at a mountain of wheat that threatened to burst the guts of the building's massive atrium lobby, and spewing out the grain and chaff onto Fifty-third Street and Lexington Avenue. I remember thinking about what would happen if one unlucky person tripped or miscalculated—surely the casualty would be duly scraped off the revolving door and thrown into a recycling bin by a security guard to keep the flow going.

But the doors kept spinning without a mishap, and then it was over. Just fifteen minutes was all it took to empty the place. The interlude was long enough to give me a chance to think about the wisdom of flextime, satellite offices, and the seven-day weekend. And that, I would love to say, was when I decided to dump out on the Reliance deal.

It would make a better story, I realize now, if the exodus had been the enzyme that precipitated the catalysis, but the Semco board was the catalyst.

I was merely the messenger on my way into the Citicorp Center that day to inform the Reliance lawyers that the deal was off, scuttled by Clovis Bojikian's question when the board met for a final discussion of the takeover. "Excuse me, I know we've looked at all the angles, and that we will grow by three times with this acquisition, but just indulge me with one response," he paused and asked: "Why is it really that we are doing this?" Several hours later, most of them spent in heated discussion, we decided that Semco had been about to acquire Reliance merely for the sake of growth. Not a good enough reason. I would go to New York to deliver the news personally. And that was that.

When I informed the Reliance team that we were pulling out, they politely suggested that Semco should add a psychiatrist to its board. An unusually temperate response considering the months of negotiations that had gone down the drain. I'm biased, of course, but I think we'd be certified as soundly, sustainably out of control—in both practice and theory.

INDEX

self-management, 160–71
trust as value, 117–23
truthfulness as value, 136–40
turnover, 78
worker representation groups,
71–72
workers' garden, 59–60
SemcoBAC, 14
Semco Econsult, 216–17
Semco Foundation
function of, 137
Lumiar (Institute for Advanced Learning), 80–81
SemcoHR, 15
Semco Johnson Controls, 14–15
SemcoRGIS, 160–62
flexibility, 26
function of, 15
growth of, 97–98
Semco Ventures
function of, 15
and high-tech bust, 196–97
Semler, Antonio Curt, 10, 182
Semler, Ricardo, takes over Semco, 11
Semler & Company, 10
Seven-day weekend
meaning of, xii-xiii
and Semco, xii-xiii
Sexual harassment, 130
Shop workers, garden for, 59–60
Singer, Eugenio, 216
Singer Sewing Machines, 144, 158
Situational leadership, 198–200
Social balance sheets, 102
Stock/stock options, as benefit option,
178
Strand bookstore, 4
Stress, 46–51
basic cause, 46, 49
everyday sources of, 49–51
and lateness, 47–49
negative effects of, 47
and organizational expectations,
46–47
Strikes, 70
Success
Barometer, 99–103
in business context, 90
and growth of business, 89–98
wealth versus calling, 104–6
Success fee, 62

Sustainable organization, 164–65
Symbiosis, modern need for, 26
Synergy, 16

Talents of individuals. See Reservoir of
talent
Teams, size of, 165–66
Technology, as barrier to free time,
23–25
Telecommuting
false assumptions about, 29–30
future view, 30, 31
prevalence of, 30
Tests, preemployment, 149
Thatcher, Margaret, 164
Theft, Semco response to, 167–68
Three Tenors, 117
Tinoco, Rafael, 79–80
Traditional companies, compared with
Semco, 8–9
Training. See Education/training
Tribalism
function of, 141–42
and hiring practices, 153
negative aspects, 156–57
Trust, 117–23
Trustees. See Board of trustees
Truthfulness
dissent, 136–40
and ethics, 122–23
and information sharing, 125–36
lack of, Semco example, 119–20
mistakes, acknowledgment of,
128–29
and peer control, 118–19
Turnover, Semco, 78

United Parcel Service (UPS), 99
Unilever, 16
Up 'n' Down Pay program, 51–52
U.S. Postal Service, 99, 167

Values, versus profits, Semco example,
93–96
Varig, 1
Vendramim, Joao, 145, 201
Verizon, 226
Vienna Philharmonic, 92
Violi, Jose, 83–84, 88, 94–95, 196
Violin, Celso, 175
Volvo, 92